Preaching as Paying Attention

Theological Reflection in the Pulpit

EDWARD FOLEY, CAPUCHIN

LITURGY
TRAINING
PUBLICATIONS

Nihil Obstat
Rev. Mr. Daniel G. Welter, JD
Chancellor
Archdiocese of Chicago
April 19, 2021

Imprimatur
Most Rev. Robert G. Casey
Vicar General
Archdiocese of Chicago
April 19, 2021

The *Nihil Obstat* and *Imprimatur* are declarations that the material is free from doctrinal or moral error, and thus is granted permission to publish in accordance with c. 827. No legal responsibility is assumed by the grant of this permission. No implication is contained herein that those who have granted the *Nihil Obstat* and *Imprimatur* agree with the content, opinions, or statements expressed.

The poem "Words" by Anne Sexton is reprinted by permission of SLL/Sterling Lord Literistic, Inc. Copyright Linda Gray Sexton and Loring Conant, Jr. 1981. "The Lectern," by Malcolm Guite is reprinted by permission of Norwich: Canterbury Press.

This book was edited by Victoria M. Tufano. Michael A. Dodd was the production editor, Anna Manhart was the designer, and Mark Hollopeter was the production artist.

Cover art: Shutterstock/AlexGreenArt

25 24 23 22 21   1 2 3 4 5

Printed in the United States of America

Library of Congress Control Number: 2021931805

ISBN: 978-1-61671-637-0

PPA

DEDICATED TO

Herbert, Dianne, Gary, and Bob

CONTENTS

INTRODUCTION

I t definitely was not my first passion when I entered full-time ministry. As a young cleric, pastoral counseling seemed more satisfying, and issues of liturgical music more interesting to explore, than homiletics. While I did preach regularly—sometimes six or seven times a week as a fledgling campus minster—it was more an integral part of the assignment rather than a source of particular delight or fervor. That perception has changed radically over the decades, and preaching has emerged as a defining ministerial practice for me. What triggered that change was not further theological studies, years of teaching liturgy, nor the innumerable student homilies I heard from ordination candidates practicing their presiding skills. Rather, the transformation occurred because of an immersion in the field of practical theology and the importance it gives to theological reflection.

Theological reflection must have been part of my seminary training, but frankly I do not remember it. This was not a skill I explicitly explored; many other frameworks appeared more valuable for my teaching and pastoral work. All of that changed when colleagues introduced me to the field of practical theology. This approach values human experience as much as dogmas or theories in the process of theologizing. Rather than simply applying some presumably universal ethic or spirituality in every situation that comes along, practical theology requires placing the specifics of each circumstance into critical dialogue with established principles and traditional teachings.

In order to achieve a fruitful dialogue between theory and practice, it is essential to pay attention. This means not only attending to Church teaching, tradition, and Scripture but also paying attention with equal intensity to people and the context of their lives. Such attentiveness is important if we are going to grow in the awareness of how God is acting in our personal histories and those of the folk we accompany. "Theological reflection" is a fancy name for considering how God is present to us in the great and small moments of life and for discovering who that presence invites us to be.

It eventually dawned on me that preaching is one of our most public and potent ways to engage in this sacred attending. In the context of worship, the official liturgy of the Church meets the liturgy of people's lives. That unique encounter provides a distinctively graced arena for discerning how God's Spirit works in our individual and collective existence. It is also one of the most exposed and challenging ventures ministers dare undertake.

In the ensuing pages, I share many of the ways people have taught me to pay attention for the sake of more effective preaching. These include scores of ideas and frameworks from different disciplines that have enhanced my homilizing. Besides exploring these concepts and constructions, I illustrate their adaptability to preaching. Thus, while there is a chapter on employing the sciences, the whole volume is punctuated with insights and discoveries from multiple scientific fields. Consult the entries *science* and *scientists* in the index for some appreciation of how they have become integrated into my homilizing. Similarly, the excursion into the arts and poetry is not confined to that one chapter. Rather, examples from literature and film, from classical traditions and pop culture, are strewn throughout the book. The index bears this out as well. Even the Roman Missal, which seems such familiar territory for preachers, is reexamined in the language of John Hanson Mitchell as the "undiscovered country of the nearby." This approach reflects my own preaching style, which draws upon a wide array of resources in this public ministry of attending. There is also serious attention to language craft here. The final chapter provides some of the rhetorical and scientific reasoning behind this strategy. While the style I employ here might not be one you find comfortable using with your communities, the thinking behind the writing is that our words have an impact. Metaphors make a difference. Language that refers to sensory experience prompts the attention of our hearers much more than didactic or dogmatic speech.

While it seems presumptuous to offer sample homilies for this very contextual form of ministry, honesty requires that I demonstrate to some degree how these ideas and strategies actually come together. The compromise here is a series of excerpts from my own preaching, mostly delivered at Old St. Patrick's Church in downtown Chicago. None of these selections were constructed for this book, and all were part of an actual preaching event. The full texts of these homilies are posted at edwardfoleycapuchin.org. The excerpts in this volume are positioned within a discussion of a specific resource or genre—such as the Elephant Listening Project at Cornell University or the movie *Frozen*—that is intended to offer some enhanced background for understanding the larger sermon.

As in preaching, such a writing venture requires honest feedback and critique. I have been honored by many individuals and groups who have commented on various segments of this work or even pored over the whole manuscript with care. Particular thanks are due to Dr. Lilith Usog, Dr. Patricia Eldred, Mary Prete, Virgil Funk, Prof. Dianne Bergant, Dr. Jack Tucek, and Capuchin friar Keith Clark. I am also grateful to the Gay+ group at Old St. Patrick's Church, as well as the students enrolled in my Preaching and the Sciences course at Catholic Theological Union for their input on the project.

Thank you also to Liturgy Training Publications, especially Victoria Tufano and Deanna Keefe, for initiating this project and graciously guiding it to completion.

This publication was made possible through the support of a grant from the John Templeton Foundation. The opinions expressed in this publication are those of the author and do not necessarily reflect the views of the John Templeton Foundation.

Finally, I offer profound thanks to the four colleagues at Catholic Theological Union who introduced and mentored me in practical theology: Herbert Anderson, Dianne Bergant, Gary Riebe-Estrella, and Robert Schreiter. It is to the four of them I dedicate this volume as a small gesture of gratitude and esteem.

Edward Foley, Capuchin
Pentecost, 2020

The Journey into Attending

Attention is the only thing that guarantees insight.

~Michelle Dean

It is something you have heard before, maybe repeatedly, possibly from a teacher or a coach or even a parent: "Now, pay attention!" This cautionary phrase sometimes signaled the importance of a historical fact or mathematical equation that was critical to remember for an upcoming test. Other times it was a prelude to the demonstration of a tricky technique or key maneuver that could improve your jump shot or straighten out your golf swing. In the presence of sharp cutlery or power tools, it probably flagged a safety tactic that could keep you from slicing off a finger or discharging a nail gun in the direction of your coworker. Now, pay attention!

Lagging attention spans, especially among children, has been a topic of concern and even heated debate in the medical community for decades. The condition known as attention deficit hyperactivity disorder (ADHD) is the most commonly diagnosed and repeatedly misdiagnosed mental disorder in children and adolescents. Educators and physicians have labored mightily to help students cope with this condition, employing everything from informed instructional strategies to potent drugs. The concern that underdeveloped attention skills in the young might affect their future productivity has sometimes prompted bizarre responses. Recently there were reports that some schools in China are requiring children to wear headbands that read the students' brainwaves. They generate a light on the front of the headband, with different colors that indicate varying concentration levels in each student. In addition, teachers can access the results on a smartphone app. I suspect that most preachers would not like the results if members of our assemblies donned such devices during our sermonizing.

Despite the research and evolving medical nomenclature, anyone who has spent time in the classroom or the pulpit knows that the lack of attention is not a new issue. While it is patently false that, as widely reported, the attention span of today's adults has declined below that of goldfish, it is true that we exist in an environment laced with constant distractions. In the midst of our multitasking, we often fail to see which of the elements we are juggling are most deserving of attention. In the process, we can not only jeopardize our physical safety but also blunt our capacity to recognize beauty. More profoundly, we might leave unrecognized the Christ in our midst or forget to ponder how God might be present in the momentary chaos of our lives. Paying attention is a necessary skill for effectively negotiating the daily pandemonium that confronts us. It is also a discipline, even a virtue, that preachers need to cultivate if we are to accompany others into the mystery of God with integrity and grace.

Minding the Gap

As someone who has lived in a large urban environment for many years—and who has literally been mugged on more than one occasion—I have come to understand how important it is to be mindful of my location. This is true whether I am taking public transportation around the city or just walking through my own neighborhood. Even momentary distractions can be dangerous. How many times have you been bumped by someone more focused on their cell phone than where they were walking? Living, as we do, in an era of great freedom but also much random violence, we are bombarded with safety instructions, digital alerts, and foreboding advisories. Overhead highway signs warn of the dangers of texting and driving. Airports and other public venues blare cautionary announcements such as "see something, say something." One of the most iconic cautions in service of personal safety is that omnipresent sign throughout the London Underground warning travelers to "mind the gap!"

It is not only the pursuit of personal or collective safety, however, that nudges us to stay alert. This skill must also be cultivated if and when we decide to embark on the quest for beauty. Painters, poets, and artists of every stripe repeatedly astonish us with their ability to observe some landscape or capture some moment that the rest of us hardly notice. Maybe that is what motivated the French-American painter-sculptor Marcel Duchamp to remark that "the only thing that is not art is inattention." Some gifted souls, such as the impressionist painter Claude Monet, have the uncanny ability to revisit the same scene over and over again, each time with fresh perspectives and wondrous insights. A favorite example is Monet's series of "wheat stack" paintings, six of which are part of the collection at the Art Institute of Chicago. It is endlessly fascinating to see these works side by side, inviting us into the artist's discerning gaze as he explores these mundane objects through mutating sunlight and changing seasons. Imagine the delight if one could experience all twenty-five of Monet's paintings in this series—currently scattered around the world's great museums—in one breath-taking exhibition.

Equally wondrous for me are the singular powers of observation exercised by writers, especially poets. A personal favorite who epitomizes this gift is Mary Oliver, confessing in one of her poems that she does not know what prayer is but she does know how to pay attention. She is a particularly astute observer of nature and was once described in an interview published in the *New York Times* as the kind of poet who most days walks the woods with her dog and her notepad. I am both awed and astonished by the images she crafts from her studied surveillance of the natural world. Her poems are populated with loons and geese, insects and stars, ponds and rain. There is even a collection about dogs, which she once described as "perfect companions [since] they don't speak!" Her startling powers of observation often stop me in my tracks, at once compelling me to ask, "How could she have seen that?" and to wonder, "How could I have missed noticing it in the first place?"

While preachers are not formed to be award-winning poets or best-selling authors, preaching is nonetheless a particular and crucial art form, as is ministry itself. This clearly is not a new idea. In the twelfth century the French theologian Alain de Lille had penned the

Ars praedicandi (Latin, "the art of preaching"), which spawned a whole genre of manuals and commentaries on the preaching arts that continues to our own day.

While there are certainly natural gifts of voice and ease that dispose some more readily than others for this ministry, preachers, like Christians, are made, not born. Fostering this gift requires a dedication and discipline parallel to that required of sculptors or other artisans. South African theologian Daniël Louw contends that preaching is fundamentally the art of "poetic seeing." This cannot be achieved through nonchalant looking or random observation, but only by intention and practice. It is only then, as Louw instructs, that preachers are capable of "seeing the unseen" and thus are better equipped for accompanying their communities into the holy mysteries. Notably, learning not only what to look at but also how to gaze with curiosity and respect is required for shaping a preaching path capable of leading to a revelatory art. To rephrase Duchamp's caution noted above, studied inattention does not produce art.

Seeing "As" Rather Than Seeing "That"

In late nineteenth-century Germany, an unnamed illustrator created an ambiguous image that became a famous touchpoint in philosophical discourse. It presents a figure that from one perspective appears to be a duck yet from another angle seems to be a rabbit. The image was made famous by the Austrian philosopher Ludwig Wittgenstein. He employed it to illustrate two different ways of seeing, which he labeled "seeing that" and "seeing as." Wittgenstein used "seeing as" to mean "noticing

an aspect." For example, when first viewing this iconic drawing we might say, "It's a duck." After closer scrutiny, however, we might say, "Oh, now I see; the duck's beak is actually a rabbit's ears." According to Wittgenstein, this dawning awareness is appropriately understood as a change in our viewpoint or "aspect," since nothing has physically changed in the illustration nor in our physiology of seeing. The only thing that has changed is our perception. We are no longer simply "seeing that" it is a duck, but understanding that, by changing our point of view, we can also see it "as" a rabbit.

Many of us have had similar experiences. Usually, the more self-reflective we become the more we develop the capacity to perceive more than one aspect of a situation. It starts with a basic awareness "that" some event has occurred, which on the surface does not seem that unusual or notable. Upon closer scrutiny, however, we begin to perceive it "as" something else and detect an originally hidden aspect. For example, we see "that" a coworker is unusually diligent and cheerful at work. After picking up on a few other hints, however, we only later perceive her "as" newly engaged, and that she will be moving to a new city where she has secured an even better job. Or we observe "that" an unexpected candidate is appointed to a key position in city government. With the help of investigative news reporting, however, we eventually begin to see the person "as" the son of a major donor to the mayor and the beneficiary of political nepotism. Closer to home, VIRTUS training and other programs to help provide safe environments for children train ministers not simply to see "that" an adult is being kind or has taken special interest in a child or other vulnerable person. Rather, this training primes us to be vigilant that such interest might in some cases be seen "as" a form of grooming or seduction that could lead to inappropriate behavior. More broadly, developing a mature Gospel spirituality challenges believers not only to see "that" people are poor or marginalized or excluded from circles of power and care, but to honor such people "as" unique reflections of the divine image and God's beloved who are deserving of respect and loving regard.

Jesus was always "noticing an aspect" and consequently perceiving underlying realities that others carelessly ignored. Consider, for instance, the case of the Samaritan woman in the Gospel of John (4:4–42). Where others saw "that" she had more husbands than was tolerable, and so they shunned and avoided her, Jesus saw her "as" a potential disciple, remarkably open to his revelation. By seeing her "as" more than her marital status, Jesus enabled this celebrated divorcée to share his "living water" with the whole of her village. Through her, those residents came to have faith in Jesus as Lord and Savior. Similarly, her coming to perceive "that" Jesus was not just a lost Jew who had wandered into Samaritan territory, but "as" an unexpected yet authentic prophet enabled her own transformation into a local apostle and messenger of good news.

A parallel point could be made about Jesus' encounter with Zacchaeus (Luke 19:1–10), his keen understanding of the role of John the Baptist (Matthew 11:7–14), or his grateful gaze on the woman who anointed him in view of his impending death (Mark 14:3–9). Jesus was divinely gifted to see past the surface or the social stigma and encounter each individual as a unique and treasured revelation of God. Furthermore, it was not only people that Jesus could perceive through the inner eyes of his sacred heart. As multiple authors have noted, Jesus was also an astute observer of nature with a deep appreciation of how the mundane realities that populated the lives of ordinary folk were in reality omens of the in-breaking of God's reign. His speech is peppered with references to sparrows and mustard seeds, flour and coins, lilies and foxes, yeast and fig trees. Each of these natural phenomena had the potential to trigger a change in aspect and lead believers deeper into holy mystery. In many respects, Jesus' culminating revelation about the gift of his enduring presence announced at the Last Supper is a mandate to look beyond the physical aspects of bread and wine and to perceive them "as" his very body and the cup of the covenant in his blood.

Developing our abilities to grasp more than one aspect of an individual or a situation is essential for people of faith. It is only by growing in this capacity that we are able to see with the eyes of Holy Wisdom and not simply as the world sees. The preaching event is an essential aid to this development. Through our careful exegesis of ancient texts and contemporary contexts, we hold up a revelatory mirror to the congregation, uncover how the Gospels are strewn with such stories of transformation, and announce that such is also possible for us.

A revered Easter text that invites such preaching is Luke's unique tale of the disciples on the road to Emmaus. The about-face that Cleopas and his companion experienced in that event transpired because something triggered a change of aspect: the ability not only to perceive "that" a stranger had crossed their path, but also to recognize the stranger "as" the risen Lord. In my own preaching on that text, I once used the work of neurologist Oliver Sacks and his work on various kinds of blindness as a way to plumb some of its meaning. People with different kinds of blindness have distinct strategies for recognizing even their closest family members, whose faces can be a complete mystery to them. The disciples on that Emmaus highway also practiced a strategy—one I believe they learned from Jesus—that prompted their changed aspect and subsequent ability to perceive the risen Lord in their midst: they extended hospitality to a complete stranger. It is a Jesus practice we can exercise as well, one that promises a renewed ability to perceive the presence of God in the face of every child, woman, and man.

Luke 24:13–35. Two disciples on the Road to Emmaus

In his book *The Mind's Eye*, the neurologist Oliver Sacks considers many different kinds of blindness and explains how people can be sight impaired in different ways for different reasons: birth defect, accident, injury, or disease. While we are familiar with obvious forms of blindness, Sacks takes us deeper into the phenomenon. For example, people with "object agnosia" cannot recognize common objects like their own car, even though their vision is otherwise normal. Startling for me was the condition known as prosopagnosia, which is the inability to recognize faces: even of close family members. Sacks himself suffers from this condition. He and others outline multiple coping mechanisms folk with this disorder employ. Sometimes they just introduce themselves and hope that others will automatically do the same. Other times folk employ extra-facial clues such as the sound of one's voice, hairstyle, glasses, or even their sense of smell to enable recognition.

So what is the key to recognizing the Risen one in our midst? What triggered a change of aspect in the two disciples fleeing Jerusalem that prompted their 180-degree turn and hightailing it back to Jerusalem? Was it the way Jesus unpacked the Scriptures, or held his cutlery, or broke the bread so distinctly? To my mind's eye, there was something else. Beyond whatever love they had for their presumably dead teacher, beyond whatever grief or fear overcame them, they instinctively performed a Jesus gesture: they opened their lives to the stranger, offered him welcome, and invited him into their company. Charity, hospitality, and care for the stranger were unassailable triggers, both then and now, for recognizing the Risen Lord.

Homily excerpt, Third Sunday of Easter, Year A

Preaching through Paying Attention

Preaching can rightly be understood as a form of witness that is birthed through a rich and multifaceted process of paying attention, even during the homiletic event. For example, when someone in the congregation experiences a distressing medical event—something that has happened to many a preacher, including me—droning on with our prepared text is not acceptable. Ministering from the pulpit means that we stay present to the moment. In a medical emergency it translates into acknowledging the distress, mustering congregants to help, prayerfully calming the assembly through the incident, and to the extent possible recalibrating the preaching if and when it is resumed. While an unwanted interruption, such a situation ultimately can be transformed into a distinctive and memorable exercise of pastoral care. On a less dramatic level, in the ordinary course of our preaching we need to monitor the reception of our words in real time. Restless children, drooping eyelids, the rustle of bulletins, and a spate of coughing in the midst of our sermonizing are only ignored at our peril.

Furthermore, preaching requires much beyond paying attention in the moment. It is a ministerial event that is honed out of the cultivated practice of holy vigilance: of seeing "as" commissioned heralds of the Word. This structured alertness is necessary because of the breadth of events and sources, issues and individuals that shape the terrain from which our homilizing must emerge. Over the years, my colleague and gifted theologian Stephen Bevans has helped me understand that all theology is contextual. Similarly, all preaching must be contextual. That does not mean that our words are only about our neighborhood environment, local politics, and parish issues. Rather, in today's digitized and interconnected global village, we require some broader awareness of the sweeping economic, political, and social tides that lap against our local shores. Furthermore, as Catholic Christians, we have committed ourselves to being engaged participants in a universal Church. Consequently, through baptism we have implicitly accepted the challenge of being missionary disciples in our ever-changing world. As Pope Francis reminds us, we are called to new forms of evangelization in this liquid environment, "capable of shedding light on . . . news ways of relating to God, to others and to the world around us" (*The Joy of the Gospel,* 74).

This is a daunting task for believers and especially for preachers. For the latter, it requires a gift that might be described as compound seeing. This image is borrowed from the science of entomology, whose researchers have discovered that most insects have compound eyes. These amazing organs are composed of hundreds or even thousands of facets or optical units, every one facing a slightly different direction. Each of these visual modules filters a distinctive piece of optic data that is transmitted to the brain.

The insect brain gathers these like individual tiles in a large mosaic and is subsequently able to generate a surprisingly complete image of its environment. Some of these creatures can produce an almost 360-degree picture of their surroundings.

Compound seeing is an appropriate metaphor for the kind of vision twenty-first-century disciples and especially homilists require. What particularly intrigues me about this fascinating revelation from the world of nature is that no single optic unit in the compound eye is capable of producing anything close to an adequate portrait of an insect's surroundings. It is only when the individual facets are fused together in the creature's brain that a comprehensive view emerges. Similarly, I contend, preachers who focus only on one "optic unit" or resource in constructing the homiletic mosaic—be it the lectionary or the liturgy, poetry or politics—will have a deficient grasp of the assembly's context, and the ensuing homily will be proportionally impaired.

Admittedly, no preacher can possibly attend to every possible local and global current that might be folded into the homiletic mosaic. Such is not humanly possible, even if a minister's full-time job were preparing a single Sunday homily each week. No one I know has that luxury. The good news, however, is that preachers do not have to dip into every theological larder, exploit every literary stockpile, or utilize every current event for each outing into the pulpit. Rather, the task is first to cultivate an openness to and an appreciation of the cornucopia of sources available for nourishing the germinating process that can be harvested over time. Being aware of the vastness of this potential harvest even before its gathering is essential for developing a long-term pathway towards an effective homily. While these riches naturally include the usual suspects, such as the lectionary readings, liturgical texts, the feast or season being celebrated, and Church teaching, pastoring the Word in this era of massive disaffiliation requires much more.

It is no longer news that people in the United States and other countries, especially in North America and Europe, are leaving established religious institutions in droves. This is especially true of emerging and young adults between the ages of eighteen and thirty-five. The Roman Catholic Church is not immune to this exodus. Attending Sunday Mass, once presumed to be obligatory for Roman Catholics under pain of mortal sin, has become in many places an occasional event that folks attend with notable irregularity. Those who do attend are often unfamiliar with Bible study, the spirituality of the liturgy, and even contemporary Church teaching. While preaching can certainly aid their appreciation of these treasures, such churchly resources are not always effective launching points for preaching, as they often seem far removed from the anxieties and elations that daily greet the baptized. Even Pope Francis suggests that it is sometimes useful to begin preaching with some fact or story rather than launching into doctrine or Scripture. This is symptomatic of what the pope frames as keeping "an ear to the people" and developing an authentic sensitivity for what is really going on in their lives (*The Joy of the Gospel,* 155). Pope Francis also underscores the problem that occurs when preachers become so accustomed to their own language that they instinctively presume that everyone else naturally understands it (*The Joy of the Gospel,* 157). Preachers also risk losing the assembly if they are only in dialogue with sources that are personally appealing or nourishing. We have to cast our horizons further into their field of vision.

Seeing the Other Side

One of the unforeseen benefits of compound seeing is not only the ability to scour multiple sources for our homiletic endeavors but also the invitation to grasp and preach different sides of the same issue. This capacity is related to a critical aspect of human development. In recent decades neuroscientists have studied the ability of people, especially children, to perceive that others have opinions or feelings or beliefs that are different from their own. This is a particularly important form of "seeing as." The technical term for this concept is "theory of mind." The noted neurobiologist Robert Sapolsky succinctly describes what the absence of this theory of mind looks like:

> A two-year-old and an adult see a cookie placed in box A. The adult leaves, and the researcher switches the cookie to box B. [The researcher then asks] the child, "When that person comes back, where will he look for the cookie?" Box B—the child knows it's there and thus everyone knows [it's there]. Around age three or four the child can reason, "They'll think it's in A, even though I know it's in B." Shazam: "theory of mind." (Sapolsky 2017, 177–178)

This ability ordinarily develops in us over time and is considered essential by healthcare professionals for effectively navigating the complexities of everyday social interactions. Adolescence and emerging adulthood are particularly important periods for growing in this skill. An inability to understand that others think or feel or believe differently than we could be indicative of an extremely sheltered existence or some psychological disorder.

The unfolding ability to recognize differing opinions and even worldviews in others is crucial for healthy living. By itself, however, it is an insufficient rudder for civil and even peaceable social navigation. All too often, today's airwaves are filled with stories of intolerance and even extreme violence perpetrated upon individuals or groups precisely because they are perceived to think or believe or love differently. Thus, the ability to distinguish that others perceive life differently than we do must be tempered by pairing it with an essential sibling: empathy.

> Empathy is seeing with the eyes of another, listening with the ears of another, and feeling with the heart of another.
>
> Alfred Adler

A former colleague memorably described empathy as "your heart in my chest." This image keenly underscores that empathy is not simply the ability to recognize that you might be experiencing something different from me. It also entails the capacity to resonate with that experience and the accompanying emotions. True empathy, however, does not presume that we necessarily adopt the worldviews, assumptions, or deeply held convictions of the other in this compassionate exchange. For example, my empathizing with a Muslim woman who has been victimized because she wears a hijab in public does not require me to assent to the core beliefs of Islam. It does, however, necessitate a degree of respect for this woman's human dignity and her right to embrace the values and spiritualities that allow her and her community to flourish. It requires, at least momentarily, seeing "as" she sees and experiencing "as" she experiences.

The pairing of theory of mind with empathy can nurture a third sibling: tolerance. This often-misunderstood virtue is often thought to imply agreeing with another's ideas or actions. Tolerance, however, is almost the opposite. As philosopher Rainer Forst explains, toleration is a conditional acceptance of beliefs or practices that one considers wrong, but without feeling compelled to prohibit or constrain them (Forst 2012). Thus, it is a momentary "seeing as." This does not mean that a mature capacity to discern differences joined with empathy and tolerance is devoid of any moral compass. Ethical judgments are certainly necessary when encountering practices and principles that we might find unfamiliar and even objectionable. Unfortunately, however, the human penchant for judgment is so instinctive and nearly instantaneous that we frequently evaluate situations, people, and practices without ever fully attending to them. James and Evelyn Whitehead, wise practical theologians, counsel that a necessary self-restraint in the process of attending to another is the ability to suspend judgment. This is valuable counsel for those engaged in ministry, including preaching. Persistent finger wagging from the pulpit rooted in our own instinctual biases "will cease to have 'the fragrance of the Gospel'" (*The Joy of the Gospel*, 39).

For the thoughtful preacher, these three siblings—a mature ability to recognize difference, empathy, and tolerance—are important, even necessary, skills to cultivate. Pondering Pope Francis' caution about preachers becoming mired in their own language, we also realize that there is a parallel danger of becoming bogged down in our own social, political, and theological worldviews. In our increasingly pluralistic and polarized society, the inability of a homilist both to recognize the often widely differing cultural and religious perspectives of the baptized, and to do so with empathy and tolerance, has the potential to reduce the homily to a journey into the preacher's mind rather than into the mystery of God.

This turn takes us to the very heart of our definition of a homily. If the homily is not simply a speech inserted into the liturgy but is itself a liturgical act, then like all liturgy, it is something done by Christ, head and members (*Constitution on the Sacred Liturgy,* 7). Thus, from a theological perspective the assembly is not the "object" of the preaching, or the one "acted upon." Similarly, the person standing in the pulpit is not the primary "subject"—or the one who acts—in the event. Rather, preaching, like the liturgy itself, is an encounter between God and the assembly, which the homilist is commissioned to facilitate. This means that the assembly is dogmatically defined as one of the subjects of the homiletic discourse. This seems to resonate with Pope Francis' understanding of the homily as a dialogue between God and believers that requires "not just the two who dialogue but also an intermediary" (*The Joy of the Gospel,* 144). Thus, I have come to conceive of the homily as a ritual conversation between God and the liturgical assembly—a conversation that announces God's reign as revealed in Jesus Christ through the mediation of a preacher. The preacher facilitates this encounter by offering a credible and imaginative interpretation of the in-breaking of God's reign for Christian living—in sustained dialogue with the lives of the faithful—that draws upon the whole of the liturgy, especially the lectionary texts, in the context of a particular community at a prescribed moment of their shared life. The rest of this volume will spend time excavating that definition in accessible and tangible ways. For now, the key point is that cultivating the ability to discern the differing beliefs of others, combined with empathy and tolerance, are essential if the preacher hopes to further a fruitful, life-giving dialogue between God and those who constitute our liturgical assemblies.

As I was discussing these ideas with a collaborator who self-identifies as gay, he raised a caution about the language of "tolerance" often used

in regard to those perceived as "other." He commented, somewhat pointedly, that he was tired of being tolerated by society in general and the
Church in particular. "When am I going to be valued?" he asked. "When
am I going to be loved?" His questions stopped me in my tracks. As
preachers, our capacity to be discerning, empathetic, and tolerant are
necessary and natural virtues. As Christians, however, they must equip
us to do what my friend felt was too often lacking. Discernment, empathy, and tolerance must enable us to fulfill the two great commandments: love of God and a palpable love of our diverse and sometimes
bewildering neighbors.

As preachers, we are charged with helping people connect the dots
in their lives and make sense out of them through the mediation of
Christ and his Spirit. We cannot connect the dots for them. As an aging
Caucasian male cleric, I am not in a position to know the joys and sorrows that inhabit the life of an adolescent Latinx or a middle-aged
African American parent. In order for these and other members of the
faithful to achieve their own sacred connectedness, those commissioned
to preach are called to an awareness of and openness to the range of
questions and issues—the "dots"—that permeate people's lives. This
requires not only an appreciation "that" the members of our assemblies
might think or believe differently than those of us who preach, but also
a willingness, at least momentarily, to think and believe "as" they do in
order to facilitate their holy conversation with the God of Jesus Christ.
In the process, we communicate not only God's enduring love for them,
but also our own.

From Novice to Expert

Paying attention to everything that is necessary for healthy living is
demanding; paying attention for life in the Spirit is even more so. While
a few are naturally gifted in this regard, most of us require assistance in
developing the compound way of seeing, and its accompanying virtues,
essential to the preaching enterprise. This is especially true for beginning preachers.

The work of brothers Hubert and Stuart Dreyfus—one a philosopher, the other an engineer—may be helpful here. Decades ago these
two were hired by the Air Force to help the military understand how

best to train expert fighter pilots. Through their study, the Dreyfus brothers developed a model that charts skill growth through five stages: novice, advanced beginner, competent professional, proficient professional, and expert. Widely utilized in the training of professionals in fields as diverse as medicine and music, this schema is certainly not above critique. It does, however, intelligently note that, particularly at the novice and advanced beginner levels, some pre-established rules and trustworthy frameworks are essential. A generally accepted first step for progressing on the path to competency is modeling the techniques of acknowledged masters.

There are many gifted preachers and teachers of homiletics who have offered their own methods for crafting and delivering an effective homily. Rather than adding to that formidable collection by presuming to create one more technique guaranteed to produce a prize-winning sermon, there is another dependable path into the homiletic ministry that is more easily integrated with the whole ministerial enterprise. It is also an indispensable spiritual exercise no matter where we are on the continuum between neophyte and guru. An extensively employed approach for teaching the practices of ministry—both lay and ordained—is theological reflection. I consider this an approach or path rather than one more among many methods and even definitions for engaging in this process. Quite frankly, there is no one correct way to do it.

Well known, for example, is the "see-judge-act" approach developed by Cardinal Joseph Cardijn for Young Christian Workers in Belgium at the beginning of the twentieth century. This technique later flourished in South America in the context of liberation theology and was eventually promoted by Pope St. John XXIII in his 1961 encyclical, *Mater et magistra* (Latin, "Mother and Teacher"). In the English-speaking world, James and Evelyn Whitehead devised the first widely accepted method of reflection designed for helping ministers arrive at theologically informed yet pastorally respectful decisions. This approach centers around the three steps of attending, asserting, and pastoral decision making (which they later nuanced as "pastoral response"). Other celebrated methods have been developed by Thomas Groome, Patricia O'Connell Killen, and John de Beer, as well as Joe Holland and Peter Henriot. These and others have made distinctive contributions to helping ministers develop this bedrock ministerial skill. I find that, in virtually all of these, what I am exploring here as "paying attention" is foundational. Various approaches emphasize differently which sources or voices take priority. However, they all seem to accentuate that theological reflection requires a kind of spiritual alertness that draws us out of ourselves and respectfully into the sphere of the other, deeply into our religious traditions and eventually out to the wider Church and world.

Theological reflection could be considered the ministerial equivalent of an idea that we explored above: seeing as. The basic contention behind this ministerial exercise and the core reason we theologically pay attention is our deep-seated belief that God's Spirit is afoot in the world and that Christ's promised Advocate abides with us. However, because of the pressing demands of daily living and the many distractions that flood our waking hours, we are not always attuned to this sacred dwelling among us. We notice "that" individuals and incidents large and small intersect with our everyday routines, and a few of them might stick in our memories or seem sufficiently notable to narrate to a friend. Nonetheless, the baptized and those who minister to them are not always spiritually attuned to how God might be acting in and through these great and small moments of our existence. Theological reflection is essentially paying attention to how and where the Holy One might be inviting us deeper into the mystery of our own baptism. It is what the thoughtful German theologian Karl Rahner understood as "the mysticism of daily living."

Earlier in this chapter the concept of "theory of mind" was presented as the human capacity to recognize that other people think or believe or feel differently than we do. Analogously, theological reflection could be envisioned as a kind of spiritual theory of mind. The Scriptures teach us that God and human beings do not always think or believe or feel the same. For example, through the prophet Isaiah God pointedly announced, "My thoughts are not your thoughts, neither are your ways my ways" (Isaiah 55:8). In this vein, theological reflection could be regarded as a holy discipline whose goal is to think and believe and feel "as" God does. Obviously, human beings cannot know the mind of God in any complete or fulsome way, but we profess that in baptism we have been graced with God's own Spirit, which is sealed in confirmation. We profess this same grace in the eucharistic prayer when invoking God's Spirit over the elements of bread and wine and over the assembly preparing to receive them. Moreover, multiple passages in the New Testament, especially in the writings of St. Paul, urge us to set our minds on higher things (Colossians 3:2), to be transformed and renew our minds as we discern the will of God (Romans 12:2), and even to take on the very mind of Christ (1 Corinthians 2:16).

> We have not received the spirit of the world but the Spirit that is from God, so that we may understand the things freely given us by God. . . . For "who has known the mind of the Lord, so as to counsel him?" But we have the mind of Christ.
>
> 1 Corinthians 2:12, 16

This psychic-spiritual transformation unfolds in the utterly commonplace, familiar terrain of our own lives that, to our astonishment, we come to see as the arena in which the Holy One calls us more deeply into divine communion.

Christian ministers are not ordained proxies for the people of God. Consequently, as preachers or other positions of ecclesial leadership, we do not substitute our reflective gifts for those of the baptized. Rather, in the shepherding and guiding offered through our preaching, we model the kind of reflective believing that every disciple who wishes to mature in their baptismal vocation needs to undertake. Thus, we cultivate the gifts of seeing "as" and strive to take on the mind of Christ. In preaching, we not only share the insights that paying attention in the Spirit has yielded for us personally but, more importantly, we invite each hearer of the Word to a similar attentiveness in their own lives. Doing so renders our preaching not only a graced moment in the Church's liturgy but also an enduring resource in the liturgy of people's own lives.

The New Apologetic

Admittedly, many forms of theological reflection are calibrated to personal goals, such as the attainment of individual wisdom or a deeper relationship with God. In some ways, Rahner's invitation to daily mysticism in the great and small moments of life confirms the richness of this approach. Other times this reflective process serves a wider purpose within a community as it aids groups of believers to come to grips with the mysterious presence of God in the midst of some crossroad or catastrophe in their collective faith life. For example, in many local churches the past decades have witnessed innumerable parish consolidations and closures, deanery restructuring, and diocesan reorganizations. While various strategies—often borrowed from the fields of organizational development or crisis management—have been profitably employed in such circumstances, they are no substitute for theological reflection. Searching for the disturbing presence of God in the midst of such upheaval is the only sure path toward sacred hope in the face of such grieving and loss.

Similarly, preaching could be understood as a form of public theological reflection. This might occur, for example, as a homilist unpacks the proclaimed good news to help a community grapple with some congregational dilemma, such as a parish closing. The liturgical context provides a key prism here for apprehending how God is at work in the current quandary. The homily places local need in dialogue with the Eucharistic revelation of Christ's presence that invites a holy communion between him and his disciples as they explore faithful pathways through the looming predicament. Such an approach to preaching as a public mode of reflecting theologically is greatly needed in our assemblies. It displays both a keen awareness of in-house needs and the pastoral wisdom to engage communal issues through the prism of the liturgy.

This understanding of preaching as a public mode of theological reflection provides a distinctively local answer to the question "for whom do we pay attention?" There is, however, another way of imagining the homiletic act as a medium for public theological reflection that answers that question in quite a different way. This alternative approach has emerged in response to a more expansive view of evangelization and mission that has evolved in Catholic thought over the past few decades. Traditional approaches to evangelization had the goal of converting people to our religion or reigniting the fervor of disaffected believers. Pope Francis, however, building on the insights of his predecessors, has broadened our understanding of the Church's missionary task by emphasizing both the "joyful" and the "witness" nature of evangelization. Transformed by our own joyful encounter with Jesus Christ, all the baptized are missioned to bring personal testimonies of his merciful message to the world. This includes witnessing Christ's presence both to those committed to furthering the in-breaking of his reign, and to those whose commitment to this baptismal vocation has waned.

Pope Francis has pushed the boundaries further, extending our evangelizing mission to those of other religions and even to those with no religious affiliation or admitted faith. The goal of such evangelizing is not to add converts or boost the head-count for the Sunday assembly, but rather to build bridges even with those who no longer or never claimed our Church as their home. It is a form of pastoral theologizing that puts the formidable spiritual and ethical resources of the Church in dialogue with the delights and sorrows of the current age. Our joyful announcement of God's mercy and hope for our sometimes-battered world may not always draw disenchanted believers or the religiously unaffiliated into our Sunday assemblies. That is not, however, the only litmus test for effective preaching as public theological reflection. Rather, our Gospel witness also has the holy purpose of presenting our Church as a credible ally in defending human dignity, promoting peace, and protecting the created world.

> As believers, we also feel close to those who do not consider themselves part of any religious tradition, yet sincerely seek the truth, goodness, and beauty which we believe have their highest expression and source in God. We consider them as precious allies in the commitment to defending human dignity, in building peaceful coexistence between peoples, and in protecting creation.
>
> Pope Francis, *The Joy of the Gospel*, 257

Our sermonizing is increasingly less a closed, internal affair. The reality in this digitized and interconnected world is that what we say in the pulpit can, for good or for ill, be easily disseminated among family and friends, absent community members, and even a global audience. A case in point is an infamous funeral homily at a Catholic Church in New Mexico during which the preacher was reported to have condemned the deceased as a sinner, lukewarm in his faith, concluding that the Lord "vomited people like [him] out of his mouth to hell." Segments of this homily, preached at a funeral attended by fewer than two hundred people in a city of about 1100 inhabits, eventually was broadcast to the world by the BBC and other international news outlets, and still lives on the internet. This is not public theological reflection, but a blatant absence of holy reflectivity that sadly erupted into a public scandal.

Australian theologian Gerald O'Collins has famously noted that a theologian is someone who watches their language in the presence of God. Preachers as public theologians, however, have a second important task here: watching our language in the presence of God's people — all of them. We do this not because we are concerned that wider audiences are eavesdropping on our preaching, but because that larger public is an increasingly important dialogue partner in our homiletic ministry. A familiar Johannine text reminds us that God has a love affair that extends far beyond the baptized; God has a love affair with the world (John 3:16). The imaginary boundary between the Sunday homily and those outside the liturgy at which it takes place is growing more porous, and not simply because of the ubiquitous recording devices carried into the worship venue. Consider the growing occurrence of intermarriage between Catholic Christians and Muslims, Sikhs, the unaffiliated, and the religiously disenfranchised. While these non-Christian spouses may not frequent weekly Eucharist, they do attend weddings, baptisms, and other occasional services.

A few years ago, I presided and preached at the funeral of a staunchly Roman Catholic grandmother and great grandmother whose children had largely disaffiliated from the Church. Her grandchildren and their partners ran the religious gamut from ardent Roman Catholic to Wiccan. This did not strike me as a moment to chastise unbelievers nor coax disenchanted baptized back into the fold. Rather, it seemed a unique opportunity not only to laud the religious convictions of a beloved grandmother but also to put the formidable resources of her faith, so deeply shared with her late husband, at the service of this polyphonic gathering. I wanted them to feel welcomed into their grandparents' faith and was compelled to preach the good news of resurrection in such a way that they could glimpse, at least momentarily, the wisdom of this treasured familial legacy.

Christian theology and preaching has a tradition of apologetics. The term has its roots in the Greek word *apologia*, a term ancient philosophers such as Aristotle understood as a type of speech employed to defend a position or action in a systematic and credible way. Christian

> ### First Reading: Acts 16:11–15, The woman named Lydia
>
> It often occurs that the person who speaks the most at a wedding or funeral is the one who knows the person at the center of the ritual the least. Most of you knew Anne better than I, but that is not to say that I didn't know her, or even know her well. For decades, I have heard her stories told and retold by her children, grandchildren, and friends. Yesterday I had the delight of sitting with some of her family again as they regaled me and each other with tales of the mite who became Anne the mighty.
>
> The online posting from a granddaughter summarized it well: she lived an epic life; she took a small gift shop and turned it into a thriving business; she fulfilled her wanderlust and traveled the world; and in her waning years, even as her mind wandered, her sense of self and her faith never did.
>
> Because of her stature in family and beyond, and because of her deep faith, the family could dip into the wisdom of the New Testament and find resonance between her life and that of Lydia from the Acts of the Apostles: a first-century entrepreneur and woman of action who opened her heart to God's Word and, by consequence, had to open her house to God's people. It is difficult to know if Lydia was a red-haired firebrand, short of stature and smart with a denarius, but I am guessing that she and Anne would have recognized each other as sisters and kindred spirits. Anne was a hearer of the Word, and as you know better than I, she and Jerry continuously opened their table, their home, their lives to those in need.
>
> Homily excerpt, Funeral for Anne, age 93

theologians starting with St. Paul have often engaged in apologetics to defend the Gospel (e.g., Philippians 1:7). St. John Newman wrote a famous defense of his nineteenth-century passage from Anglicanism to Roman Catholicism, which he titled *Apologia pro vita sua* (literally, "a defense of one's own life").

In this age of interfaith dialogue, and inspired by the example of Pope Francis, we seem poised for a "new apologetic." Francis urges the baptized to engage in joyful testimony, and to offer what he calls "a radiant and attractive witness of fraternal communion" (*The Joy of the Gospel*, 99). This is not shaming or reproaching others but raising up the beauty of our faith tradition as a light to be shared rather than a correction to be imposed. The twentieth-century spiritual writer Madeleine L'Engle luminously anticipated this new apologetic:

> We do not draw people to Christ by loudly discrediting what they believe, by telling them how wrong they are and how right we are, but by showing them a light that is so lovely that they want with all their hearts to know the source of it. (L'Engle 2016, 113)

I deeply embrace this new apologetic in my own preaching, believing that it takes us to the core of the Jesus revelation and his unflappable message of love. It also serves to build bridges rather than walls, inviting those too easily identified as religious foes to become precious allies in the quest for human dignity.

Conclusion

In his epic World War II novel *Empire of the Sun*, author J. G. Ballard gives his young protagonist Jim a front-row seat for the rise and fall of Japan during the 1940s. In one memorable scene, Jim observes brilliant flashes on the eastern horizon and instinctively shields his face with his hand. Steven Spielberg's film based on the book depicts that moment with a stunning x-ray shot, as the bones in the boy's hand become momentarily visible to him. Although he was hundreds of miles away, Jim had witnessed the atomic flash from the bombing of Nagasaki. When asked about it later on, the precocious lad surmises that the reason for the atomic blast is that "God wanted to see everything."

God not only wants to see everything, but as Christians who believe in the abiding presence of Christ's Spirit in the world today, we affirm that God does see everything. In a phrase, God is paying attention to us—all of us.

> Jim asked: "Basie, did you see the atom bomb go off? I saw the flash over Nagasaki from Nantao Stadium." "Say, kid. . . ." Basie peered at Jim, puzzled by the calm voice of this bloody-nosed boy. He took a gun rag from the rear windowsill and wiped Jim's nose. "You saw the atom bomb?" "For a whole minute, Basie. A white light covered Shanghai, stronger than the sun. I suppose God wanted to see everything." "I guess He did. That white light, Jim. Maybe I can get your picture in Life magazine."
>
> J. G. Ballard,
> *The Empire of the Sun*, 257.

The Holy One attends to believers and non-believers, to the little ones and the mighty, to each newborn in a neonatal unit and to the fragile octogenarian in hospice. The divine gaze permeates the cosmos and is focused enough to see the broken heart of an orphan and wide angled enough to witness the anguish of a warming planet.

Although preachers and other ministers cannot possibly possess anything akin to this divine optic, we are delegated to practice such holy seeing and thus learn how to pay attention with empathy and generosity. In addition, homilists are individually invited to discern how God is at work in the shadows and abandoned places of our own lives. This personal rehearsal, however, is not simply for our own benefit, but for the people of God who have elected us to this holy speaking, and for a world that craves a respectful and hopeful word. So we practice paying attention for the sake of the baptized and for the sake of the world in the hope that our homilizing will in truth be good news.

References

Ballard, J. G. 2005. *The Empire of the Sun*. New York: Simon and Schuster.

BBC News 2020. Accessed May 14, 2020. http://news.bbc.co.uk/2/hi/americas/3074245.stm.

Dreyfus, Stuart E. and Hubert L. Dreyfus. 1980. "A Five-Stage Model of the Mental Activities Involved in Directed Skill Acquisition." (February 1980). *Washington, DC: Storming Media*.

Forst, Rainer. 2012. "Toleration." In *The Stanford Encyclopedia of Philosophy*. Ed. Edward N. Zalta. https://plato.stanford.edu/archives/win2012/entries/toleration/.

Francis, Pope. 2013. Apostolic exhortation *Evangelii gaudium* (*The Joy of the Gospel*). http://w2.vatican.va/content/francesco/en/apost_exhortations/documents/papa-francesco_esortazione-ap_20131124_evangelii-gaudium.html.

L'Engle, Madeleine. (1972) 2016. *Walking on Water: Reflections on Faith and Art*. New York: Convergent Books.

O'Collins, Gerald. https://www.americamagazine.org/content/all-things/catholic-theology-today-30-questions-gerald-ocollins-sj.

Louw, Daniel. 2016. "Preaching as art (imaging the unseen) and art as homiletics (verbalizing the unseen)." *HTS Teologiese Studies/Theological Studies* 72, no. 2. http://dx.doi.org/10.4102/hts.v72i2.3826.

Rahner, Karl. 1981. "Mystical Experience and Mystical Theology." In *Theological Investigations XVII*. Trans. Margaret Kohl, 90–91. New York: Crossroad.

Sapolsky, Robert. 2017. *Behave: The Biology of Humans at Our Best and Worst*. New York: Penguin Press.

Whitehead, James and Evelyn Whitehead. 1995. *Method in Ministry*. Rev. ed. Kansas City: Sheed and Ward.

CHAPTER 2

Here Comes Everybody

Tell me what you pay attention to and I will tell you who you are.

~Jose Ortega y Gasset

The "invisible gorilla," one of the most celebrated experiments in contemporary psychology, tested the human capacity to pay attention. In what they label a "selective attention test," the designers of the experiment, Christopher Chabris and Daniel Simons, asked participants to watch a short video in which six people—two teams of three, one team wearing black shirts, the other wearing white—passed two basketballs to their teammates. At the beginning of the video, still widely available on the internet, the viewers are instructed to count how many times the players wearing white pass the basketball. Most of those participating in this experiment came up with the correct answer: the white team passed the ball fifteen times.

Then the researchers asked an unexpected second question: Did you see the gorilla? Participants often responded with blank stares or "What are you talking about?" On average, fifty percent of them never saw the person in a gorilla suit dancing through the video right in front of them. The researchers replayed the film, and there it was. In the middle of the video, as the black and white teams are passing basketballs around, the faux primate saunters into the video from the right, walks into the middle of the action, faces the camera and beats its chest a few times, then exits at the other side. It sounds crazy that such an obvious and ridiculous character could be overlooked, but I know this is possible from firsthand experience A number of years ago, a student conducted this experiment in one of my classes; multiple students and, yes, their distracted instructor missed the dancing beast.

Chabris and Simons have repeated this experiment over the years and devised others to test the prevalence of what they deemed "inattentional blindness." They concluded that when we direct our mental spotlight to something like the passing of a basketball, it leaves the rest of the world and its dancing gorillas in darkness, causing what these scientists call the "illusion of attention." We think we see the world as it is, but we often experience a striking mental blindness. In evidence of that fact, Charis and Simons have documented that experienced professional pilots do not always notice the plane blocking the runway right in front of them as they are coming in for a landing. Similarly, a police officer can miss seeing a physical assault taking place when the officer is in pursuit of a suspect in a different crime. In these and multiple other situations, the ignored data or overlooked incident was simply not what the person was looking for. Their mental spotlights were focused elsewhere, and they missed the proverbial gorilla.

It might seem outlandish to make the analogous suggestion that the assembly is some kind of invisible gorilla in the preaching event. To state the obvious: the people of God are sitting right there in front of us. How could they possibly be invisible? How could they possibly be invisible? Answering that question honestly might be disturbing; it requires burrowing deep into the nature of paying attention. The Spanish-American philosopher George Santayana once commented that familiarity breeds contempt only when it breeds inattention. Preachers might presume a certain familiarity with congregants; we see them often, regularly exchange pleasantries, and not only know their names but also their church engagement and even details of their personal lives. These random bits of information about individual congregants, however, do not always equate to knowing the heart and soul of an assembly and its diverse membership.

Inattentional blindness occurs when our mental spotlights do not have beams broad enough to cast light on the unexpected, be that the gorilla dancing through a basketball game or the transgender person sitting in the fifth pew on the left side of the church near the Mary shrine. A limited vision of our assemblies may lead us to assert, perhaps subconsciously, "I understand these people; I know who is here." This is where Santayana's caution needs to break the surface of our subconscious.

Humility-Based Ethnography

Wes Jackson is a botanist and geneticist who has taught at major universities in the United States and helped found the Land Institute. This organization is concerned with the development of agricultural patterns that are both ecologically sustainable and economically viable. As a farmer turned scientist, Jackson, along with like-minded colleagues, is concerned that decisions about our environment are too often made by people with insufficient scientific information. Nonetheless, such people forge ahead with untested policies and practices that sometimes cause more harm than good. In response to this situation, Jackson and his collaborators began a movement advocating the value of an "ignorance-based worldview." They contend that a self-awareness of what one or a group collectively does not know could prompt more caution in the scientific community. This would render them less apt to wager on untried approaches that could jeopardize the well-being of our planet.

> Imagine an ignorance-based science and technology in which practitioners would be ever conscious that we are billions of times more ignorant than knowledgeable and always will be.
>
> Wes Jackson, 2005

Jackson's proposal might sound a little harsh to the ears of committed ministers. We are not ignorant of what goes on in the lives of the people we accompany, nor are we clueless about the contexts in which we pray and preach. At the same time, we frequently are unfamiliar with the many undercurrents of faith and fear, or the exact nature of the joys and sorrows of the believers we are privileged to companion. Thus, a "humility-based" ecclesial vision seems not only appropriate but also indispensable if our preaching is to be effective in inviting the baptized into deeper communion with God and the world God loves. Such ministerial modesty will certainly enable us to "keep an ear to the people," as Pope Francis has urged.

Ethnography is a broad term that covers a wide range of methods and techniques employed to study everyday human life and practices.

Emerging from the field of anthropology in the late nineteenth century, ethnography seeks to create what the celebrated anthropologist Clifford Geertz called a "thick description" of people's daily routines and rituals. The purpose of creating such a rich and nuanced portrait of the ordinary is to acquire new understandings of why communities behave the way they do and the types of meaning they forge in the process. The methods of ethnography were originally developed in field studies by Euro-American social scientists who were interested in examining what they considered remote and exotic cultures—think pith helmets in the jungles of the Amazon. Even so, ethnographic methods were found to be so effective in producing useful data that they are now used across many disciplines and fields. Musicians have employed these techniques in the relatively recent field of ethnomusicology to understand better the means and motivations of societies in producing their distinctive musics. Educators sometimes conduct ethnographic research as a way to study students as they navigate their way through stressful social conditions such as desegregation or bullying. Certain scientists employ ethnographic approaches to examine tweets, blogs, and other forms of social communication to discern political trends or economic sentiment. Even multinational companies such as Intel and Xerox utilize these approaches to improve how they match the design and marketing of their products with their actual use by present and future customers.

It is not surprising that the insights and practices of this field have made their way into the theological arena. The groundbreaking work of Ada María Isasi-Díaz and Yolanda Tarango, *Hispanic Women: Prophetic Voice in the Church*, placed the voices of marginalized Hispanic woman at the center of their theologizing. This is not a group ordinarily tapped as a resource for thinking about what it means to be church or how to live out our baptism. Through a series of interviews and accompanying theological reflections, however, Isasi-Diaz and Tarango open the door for the rest of us to this Roman Catholic population that has lived out their faith in the shadows, often in the midst of oppression and marginalization. Ethnographic methods are increasingly deployed in theologizing about the Church. This is in reaction to what British theologian Pete Ward considers a growing "methodological laziness" when it comes to ecclesiology (Ward 2012, 4). Ward critiques the common practice of theologizing about what it does or should mean to be church based on anecdotal evidence or selective reporting of people's experience. What is missing in such work, he argues, is the same kind of scholarly rigor that theologians observe when crafting a Christology or writing about Church history.

I am not suggesting here that preachers should rush out and purchase the equivalent of a pastoral pith helmet or begin hiring social scientists to canvas our congregations. Ward's critique does suggest, however, that something more is needed for surveying our pastoral landscapes than the routine recollection of pastoral anecdotes and conversational snippets. Too often, our pastoral headlights are calibrated to illuminate what we already know or find familiar. This breeds inattentional blindness concerning the unfamiliar, often rendering invisible the wide-ranging diversity that characterizes so many of our assemblies. Even congregations of modest size that on the surface exhibit little cultural or ethnic variance can harbor surprising heterogeneity regarding age, gender, economic status, disabilities, political convictions, and even faith commitment. Nurturing an ethnographic curiosity spurs preachers to cast our ecclesial spotlights beyond the edges of our normal field of vision in order to recognize the overlooked and undervalued often hiding in our assemblies in plain sight.

Pastoral care specialist Mary Clark Moschella considers ethnography a spiritual exercise in deep listening. Echoing the wisdom of legendary New York Yankee catcher and manager Yogi Berra, she too believes "you can observe a lot by watching!" Explicitly employing the lens of theological reflection, Moschella asserts that ethnography can assist religious leaders "to engage the congregation's current faith practices in theological reflection." Ministers who mature in this practice will not simply have an ability to keep abreast of the breaking news and events in a congregation, but actually "have the eyes to see and ears to hear the faith of the gathered community" (Moschella 2008, 140). A seasoned pastor and educator, Moschella understands that such deep listening can be simultaneously enlightening and disruptive. It both edifies us with the stories of grace that abound in our midst and awakens us to uncomfortable truths also there in plain sight (Moschella 2008, 146).

> I prefer a Church which is bruised, hurting and dirty because it has been out on the streets, rather than a Church which is unhealthy from being confined and from clinging to its own security. . . . [M]y hope is that we will be moved by the fear of remaining shut up within structures which give us a false sense of security, within rules which make us harsh judges, within habits which make us feel safe, while at our door people are starving.
>
> Pope Francis, *The Joy of the Gospel*, 23

Taking the ethnographic plunge requires an adventuresome spirit. It means moving out of our comfort zones and striking out on the metaphorical road with Jesus, who was imbued with God's restless Spirit and could not seem to stay very long in one place. We are forewarned, however, that like our Lord we will probably get a little dirty and maybe even bruised in the process. That, however, is the only way we will actually get close enough to take on the proverbial smell of the sheep (see Pope Francis, *The Joy of the Gospel*, 24).

Many of our parochial contexts are already so busy, sometimes crushingly so, that we cannot imagine initiating one more committee or rounding up some deep-listening volunteers to engage in this ethnographic task. Rather, the challenge and the opportunity come through widening the spiritual spotlights of already existing groups or committees. Can a pastoral council take up the evangelizing task of mapping the local parochial terrain to better detect the peripheral voices in the community that can inform the preaching and other ministries? Does a pastoral team regularly ponder the shifting demographics in the congregation or exit trends from a faith community? Is there a liturgy committee that not only plans but invites select community members or even the whole assembly to evaluate established worship patterns over the course of the liturgical seasons? One of the most overlooked suggestions of the celebrated preaching document *Fulfilled in Your Hearing* was the development of homily preparation groups that could aid the preacher to address "the real concerns of the congregation in the homily" (106). If such a group does not exist, maybe this is the time to consider inaugurating one. Social media can be a great boon here, allowing for the development of a local preaching chatroom or an asynchronous wisdom group that can keep preachers informed without necessarily adding another appointment to everyone's overloaded schedules.

Generational Differences

One daunting aspect of the pastoral terrain is the generational range in our assemblies. While ethnic and racial differences might more easily attract our attention, in some ways the intergenerational makeup of our assemblies might be more vexing to excavate. The study of age cohorts is a relatively new phenomenon in the field of sociology. It was Norman Ryder who seized upon the significance of studying cohorts during his graduate work at Princeton. In a now classic article, Ryder argued that since cohorts are used by society to achieve "structural transformation"—for example, young adults are prominent in war, revolution, immigration, urbanization, and technological change—they should be a key factor when studying societies (Ryder 1965, 843).

Ryder's insight has spawned a revolution both inside and outside of sociology. Political operatives pour over generational data when trying to position a candidate for election. Commercial advertisers target specific age cohorts as they try to boost their bottom line. Whether it is medicine or manufacturing, groups from different generations often respond differently. There is striking evidence, for example, that from the perspective of politics or religious views, a fifty-year-old African American woman often has much more in common with her fifty-year-old Caucasian neighbor than with her own fourteen-year-old daughter. Sometimes race, ethnicity, and even denominational allegiance are trumped by age.

Recently the study of religion in the United States has begun to take seriously the impact of age cohorts on beliefs and religious practices. The Pew Forum on Religion and Public Life consistently employs generational lenses as one key factor in analyzing ethical and religious trends in the United States. For example, their study on the death penalty for people convicted of murder revealed that the greatest opposition to this practice was from eighteen- to twenty-nine-year-olds, while those aged fifty to sixty-four were the most in favor of imposing that penalty. The results of their work is readily available online. A Roman Catholic organization that regularly employs cohort frameworks for analyzing ministerial data is the Center for Applied Research in the Apostolate (CARA), affiliated with Georgetown University. Sometimes they focus their research on a specific age group, as in their study of "Young Adult Catholics in the Context of Older Catholic Generations."

There have also been a series of studies conducted over a period of years by other organizations that pay serious attention to generational differences within Roman Catholicism in the United States. In one of these, "Persistence and Change," researchers analyzed religious beliefs according to four age groups: pre–Vatican II Catholics, born in 1940 or earlier; Vatican II Catholics, born between 1941 and 1960; post–Vatican II Catholics, born between 1961 and 1978; and millennials, born between 1979 and 1993. This study demonstrates that there are some similarities across these generations. For example, less than one third of respondents across all categories in this survey rated the teaching authority claimed by the Vatican as important to them. There is also similarity across the generations when it comes to giving reasons why people do not attend Mass more often. "I'm just not a religious person" found great resonance across all four cohorts. When it came to reporting actual weekly Mass attendance, however, there were stark differences across the generations. Fifty-four percent of pre–Vatican II Catholics reported weekly attendance while only 23 percent of millennials did so. Such surveys also indicate belief gaps across the generations on topics like the existence of hell and what the Roman Catholic Church teaches about Mary.

One age group that requires our particular ethnographic attention is that of young adults who are leaving established religious institutions—including the Roman Catholic Church—in droves. The materials collected in preparation for the 2018 synod of bishops, *Young People, the Faith, and Vocational Discernment*, summarized in the working document *(instrumentum laboris)* may be a useful introduction to this work. In the chapter "Listening to Young People," it notes that "listening is the truest and boldest kind of language that young people are vehemently seeking from the church" (*Young People, the Faith, and Vocational*

> There are many priests, men and women religious, lay and professional persons, and indeed qualified young people, who can help the young with their vocational discernment. When we are called upon to help others discern their path in life, what is uppermost is the ability to listen.
>
> Pope Francis,
> *Christus vivit (Christ Is Alive)*, 291

Discernment, 65). Pope Francis acknowledged this deep need when, after the synod, he admonished that "those of us who are no longer young need to find ways of keeping close to the voices and concerns of young people" (*Christus vivit [Christ Is Alive]*, 37).

Since we have already noted the context-specific nature of all preaching, it would be presumptuous to offer advice to preachers about how to address any generational divide in your own congregations. However, the young adults who participated in the preparatory sessions for the 2018 synod do provide useful guidance for preaching to them as well as for effectively ministering across the other generations. In brief, they tell us that we need to demonstrate consistently that we are listening to them. We do not have to provide answers. Actually, it is useful not to attempt forging answers for others' dilemmas. Thinking that we can easily grasp the complexities of other people's lives and provide resolutions for them from the pulpit is a bit arrogant. Instead, our task is to create a homiletic environment in which young adults as well as others come to believe that their concerns and hopes, their struggles and joys are heard and honored. They need to hear stories about their relational struggles, student debt, and uncertain futures interwoven with enlightening Gospel narratives and inviting liturgical reflections. James and Evelyn Whitehead advise that authentic listening is confirmed by demonstrating that we have heard correctly what another has said and that we appreciate its significance to them (Whitehead and Whitehead 2014, 69). This reiterates the need for stances of tolerance, empathy, and respect that we explored in the previous chapter.

This kind of respectful attending is analogous to what we hope for in prayer. A mature Christian faith holds that in both private devotion and public worship, we encounter a God who attends to us and hears our prayer. Evidence that our prayer is heard does not come from receiving some predetermined answer. Rather, it is confirmed in the intensifying bond with the divine that God's own Spirit sustains as both confirmation and consolation in prayer. To the extent that we exemplify empathy and respect without simplistic answers in our preaching, so do we model and facilitate the holy conversation between God and believers that goes to the very heart of our definition of a homily.

Race, Ethnicity, and Them-ing

For almost a century the "gospel" for home builders and real estate investors has been summarized in the maxim "location, location, location." That secular proverb underscores the undeniable reality that, when appraising the value of a home or other property, its locale is a key factor. The proximity to schools, shopping, parks, or public transportation will increase or decrease its value in the eyes of prospective buyers depending upon their personal and social values. Similarly, living in ethnically or racially diverse neighborhood might be perceived as a benefit for some, while it is pointedly avoided by others.

Our geographic location and that of our faith communities is one important factor that frames the way we assess racial or ethnic diversity. More broadly, our social location undeniably influences our degree of awareness about diversity in society and, consequently, if and how it should be addressed in our homilizing. When living in a small town or suburban neighborhood in which there is little apparent racial or ethnic variance, we might not be motivated to grapple with the wider reality that the United States has one of the most complex cultural identities in the world. Furthermore, according to virtually every piece of census and research data, the White share of our national population is declining as Black, Hispanic, Asian, and mixed-race segments grow. Closer to home, Hispanics account for the largest segment of growth within Roman Catholicism in the United States and will soon constitute the largest single ethnic slice of that group. Acknowledging that complexity, even if it is beyond the daily experience of the preacher or the local faith community, is a critical step in the art of paying attention.

Deeply intertwined with the genealogical complexity that marks our society is the ever-present specter of racism. The United States is marked not only by many forms of diversity but also by notable polarizations across those diversities. Calling our country the "United" States seems to many at least a misnomer if not a deeply contradictory term. As recent election cycles have demonstrated, this country is acutely polarized when it comes to politics. Racism is an undeniable undercurrent in that polarization, as well as in the economic and educational gaps that mar our population. We sing at every baseball game that we are "the land of the free," and that grand dame greeting visitors in New York harbor announces welcome to the tired and poor, the "huddled masses yearning to breathe free." Nonetheless, many of our fellow citizens daily encounter social barriers and financial blocks because of the color of their skin or an unfamiliar accent. If we preach from a position of privilege because of our race, education, or ecclesial status, it may be difficult for preachers to admit that racism, as many have deemed it, is our country's original sin. The recent national and even international outrage at the death of George Floyd while in police custody in Minneapolis is an explosive reminder of the pent-up rage over this enduring sin. That the asphyxiation of one Black man while a White police officer knelt on his neck could rapidly ignite a firestorm of protests across the American landscape sadly reveals the tinderbox of injustice and oppression the African-American community has been forced to endure.

Personally I would like to think that because of my family upbringing, religious formation, and extended intercultural experiences I am not a racist. Over the years, however, I have come to accept that this deeply rooted prejudice is not simply a matter of choice. How I grapple with my biases is my only real option. Thus, as a gifted colleague has helped me understand, I am

> As a kid, I saw the 1968 version of *Planet of the Apes*. . . . Years later, I discovered an anecdote about its filming: At lunchtime, the people playing chimps and those playing gorillas ate in separate groups. . . . Humans universally make Us/Them dichotomies along lines of race, ethnicity, gender, language group, religion, age, socioeconomic status, and so on. . . . We do so with remarkable speed and neurobiological efficiency; have complex taxonomies and classifications of ways in which we denigrate Thems; do so with a versatility that ranges from the minutest of microaggression to bloodbaths of savagery; and regularly decide what is inferior about Them based on pure emotion, followed by primitive rationalizations that we mistake for rationality. Pretty depressing. . . . [W]e all carry multiple Us/Them divisions in our heads. A Them in one case can be an Us in another, and it can only take an instant for that identity to flip. Thus, there is hope that, with science's help, clannishness and xenophobia can lessen, perhaps even so much so that Hollywood-extra chimps and gorillas can break bread together.
>
> Sapolsky, 2017

a racist but hopefully not a bigot cued toward intolerance and intentional discrimination.

Contemporary sciences help us understand that such prejudice is not simply a matter of choice. We are actually hardwired to differentiate "us" from "them." Psychologists sometimes refer to this phenomenon as "them-ing." Evidence suggests that human beings have evolved to distinguish almost instantaneously our type or group from another. Research from scientists at the University of Massachusetts Amherst, for example, demonstrates that even infants, who are all born with the ability to distinguish among people from multiple races, will be better at recognizing the faces and emotional expressions of people within their own group by nine months of age. There are definite values associated with this ability that apparently evolved so that humans could associate with others perceived as safe and supportive. The downsides of this innate capacity, however, are multiple. According to the neurobiologist Robert Sapolsky, for example, by the time we are three or four years old, children already group people by race and gender. Evidence further demonstrates that children of this age have more negative views of "them," and perceive "other-race" faces as being angrier than "same-race" faces (Sapolsky 2017, 391).

Some believe that there is little hope and that racism is such a crushing reality that it will never be eradicated. In a brutally jarring book written as a letter to his fifteen-year-old son, African American author Ta-Nehisi Coates bluntly tells his first-born, "Here is what I would like for you to know: In America, it is traditional to destroy the black body—it is heritage" (Coates 2015, 103). The multiple awards heaped upon this volume attest to its deep resonance across many oppressed communities. Nobel and Pulitzer Prize winner Toni Morrison considered it required reading.

Since I am not a person of color I cannot presume to understand what Coates or Morrison feel, although I am urged to empathy, imperfect as it is. At the same time, I resonate with Pope Francis' assertion that effective preaching should not leave us trapped in negativity but always offer hope (*The Joy of the Gospel,* 159). So how does one preach hopefully in the face of systemic racism and the innate human tendency toward them-ing? One source for theological reflection and a seldom used preaching entrée here might be our foundational yet mystifying belief in the Trinity. Christians affirm that God is a unity in diversity: one divinity with three distinct persons. We also affirm that it is a mystery. It cannot be explained. The North African Doctor of the Church St. Augustine grasped that dilemma when he admitted *"Si comprehendis, non est Deus,"* roughly translated as "If you think you understand it, it's not God!" (Sermon 117).

While we cannot explain the mystery of the Trinity, that does not impede us from appreciating the pivotal revelation that proclaims the God of Jesus Christ as a community without division. To put it bluntly, while there is distinctiveness in the Godhead, there is no divine "theming" afoot in that holy triad. It is almost a cliché to announce that each of us is created in the image of God. What is less recognized, however, is that the whole of humanity is crafted in a Trinitarian image. Our racial and genealogical diversity is a holy gift that mirrors God's mysterious vastness in a way that no single individual or society or people can do. The spectrum of languages and ethnicities and cultures that the human race comprises is like an enormous gem with innumerable facets. As we rotate that jewel in the sun, each facet refracts with particular grace some aspect of the Holy One. Without this diversity we would be bereft of unique refractions of divinity and even more diminished in our ability to apprehend God. Like the Trinity, the human race is a singularity in diversity in which distinctiveness need not and must not morph into divisiveness.

Bridging the Gender Gap

While it is true that some members of the laity, both men and women, grace our pulpits from time to time, current Roman Catholic law and practice presumes that only ordained men offer homilies within public worship. Furthermore, despite the large number of married deacons in the United States, the vast majority of weekly preachers in Roman Catholic communities are unmarried. Not surprisingly, data from sources like the Pew Forum on Religion and Public life, regularly report that more women than men in the United States affirm the importance of religion in their lives. Consequently, women not only appear to pray more often than men do, they also consistently attend public worship more frequently. In one study on the gender gap in religion, Pew researchers noted that women so outnumber men in many of our churches that some parochial leaders have been experimenting with changing the décor, music, and even worship styles in order to lure more men into the assembly.

For single males such as myself, preaching across such a gender gap can be formidable. This is where married deacons may be uniquely poised to help us. With wives and daughters and even granddaughters, their familial situation positions them to hear more readily and consistently the concerns of women of various ages in our congregations. Maybe even more helpful could be their insights into the conversational approaches they have learned when effectively communicating with spouses and daughters. Fruitful communication across boundaries such as age or gender requires not only figuring out what to say but also crafting the appropriate way to say it. How do we speak effectively to our sisters in the assembly without pandering or succumbing to unhelpful caricatures about women, as though they are only or essentially maternal and supportive?

Before preaching to women it is useful to listen to them. Women who serve as pastoral associates, liturgical musicians, religious educators, and parish leaders are critical collaborators here. In ethnography they would be considered key informants. Their advice about issues that need to be tackled in our homilies, the appropriateness of examples that speak to them, and even nuances in style and language are invaluable. Ironically, the many women who share ministry with us—volunteers, part-time or even full-time staff—are seldom invited to provide advice or offer critique for those of us who regularly preach in their presence. We are squandering a great asset.

Another valuable entrée for male preachers facing this gender gap is listening to women preachers who can teach us much about gender-inclusive language, appropriate metaphors, and experiences that speak to women. A favorite resource here is the celebrated author Barbara Brown Taylor. Various surveys have frequently named her as one of the most effective preachers in the English-speaking world. She is usually the only woman on such lists. A multitude of her sermons and presentations live on the internet. While I have watched several of these, her writings have more staying power for me, as I can easily revisit them over and over again. I frequently return to *An Altar in the World*, in which Taylor ponders ordinary practices as windows to the divine. She has come to identify herself as a "detective of divinity," searching for clues of God's presence in the world and tracing down the divine tracks the Holy One has left for us to follow. These exercises in sacred ethnography are unpretentious in their language, welcoming in their familiarity, and reassuring in their accessibility. This is utterly unvarnished theological reflection to be both admired and emulated. Those of us who do not regularly listen to women preachers, teachers, or spiritual directors might find audio books an opportunity to do so. Not only is listening to them a great break from

> To make bread or love, to dig in the earth, to feed an animal or cook for a stranger—these activities require no extensive commentary, no lucid theology. All they require is someone willing to bend, reach, chop, stir. Most of these tasks are so full of pleasure that there is no need to complicate things by calling them holy. And yet these are the same activities that change lives, sometimes all at once and sometimes more slowly, the way dripping water changes stone. In a world where faith is often construed as a way of thinking, bodily practices remind the willing that faith is a way of life.
>
> Barbara Brown Taylor,
> *An Altar in the World*, xviii

the video screen and easily accomplished while driving or exercising, it also gets the sustained voice of wise women into our ears—and maybe our hearts. Listening to *An Altar in the World*, Kathleen Norris' *Amazing Grace: A Vocabulary of Faith*, or some other audio reflection from a female sage, exposes us to fresh soundwaves that can find resonance in our own public words.

We do not have to invent special homilies for women that we periodically resurrect, for example, on Mother's Day. Rather, the lectionary cycle and festival calendar offer innumerable opportunities to raise up the gifts of women for the Church. The Syrophoenician woman is emblematic of intrepid mothers who will take on even the Son of God for the sake of their children (Mark 7:24–29). Mary Magdalene, too often misidentified as a prostitute, is the first person in the Gospel of John to meet one of the basic criteria for apostleship: she is the first to encounter the Risen Lord (John 20:11–18). Then there is Junias, whom

Paul greets as an apostle (Romans 16:7), having suffered persecution and even imprisonment for the faith.

Pivotal here is how we preach about the Blessed Virgin, the most prominent woman in the liturgical calendar and our most revered saint. Sometimes preachers attend only to her submissiveness to God's will, purportedly epitomized in the celebrated yes that permitted the incarnation (Luke 1:26–38). A narrow use of this text could suggest some divine plan that presents Mary as a "yes woman," modeling an acquiescence appropriate for all truly spiritual women. Such exegetical thinness overlooks the determination, even steely faith demanded of Mary throughout a lifetime of collaboration with God. In one sermon, Barbara Brown Taylor pointedly underscores the formidable obstacles Mary faced by saying yes to God's invitation to her through the Angel Gabriel. Brown writes,

> What she does not have is a sonogram, or a husband, or an affidavit from the Holy Spirit that says, "The child really is mine. Now leave the poor girl alone." All she has is her unreasonable willingness to believe that the God who has chosen her will be part of whatever happens next—and that, apparently, is enough to make her burst into song. She does not wait to see how things will turn out first. She sings ahead of time, and all the angels with her. (*Home by Another Way*, 18)

In a recent homily on the Feast of the Immaculate Conception, I tried to address this tenacious faith by underscoring that, as a model of godly collaboration, Mary continually said yes and never no to God. While her incarnating *fiat* (Latin, "let it be done" from Luke 1:38) was the first of these, it was plainly not the last. She said yes to God through a mysterious pregnancy (Matthew 1:19), forced immigration (Matthew 2:13), hidden years (Luke 2:51), widowhood, apparent abandonment by her son (Mark 3:33–35), and especially the brutal execution of her firstborn when virtually all of the men once aligned with Jesus deserted her at the foot of the cross (John 19:25–27). She is an exemplar of resolute discipleship that needs to fire our preaching with some frequency.

Shifting Gender Boundaries

The demands implicit in preaching across the gender gap are significantly amplified by the growing awareness of sexual diversity and gender fluidity in our society and thus in our Church. This is not an issue that either seminary training or preaching labs ordinarily prepared us to address. When most of us in active ministry were in formation, it was accepted that there were two sexes, synonymous with two genders: female and male. These days, scientists recognize multiple physiological, hormonal, and chromosomal variations in humans. Some contend that there are five or six different configurations of chromosomes that occur with some regularity among humans, pointing to multiple sexes rather than just two.

While one's sex is a matter of physiology, gender is widely acknowledged as a human construct. This distinction was first addressed in the scientific literature in the mid-1950s, when psychologist John Money and his colleagues published articles that introduced the concept of "gender roles." Shortly afterwards, psychiatrist Robert Stoller examined the nature of gender identity in a series of revolutionary publications. The work of these and other specialists generated the now widely accepted theory that one's gender is not a matter of genes, hormones, or chromosomes but a product of learning, experience, and indoctrination (Diamond 2005, 592).

There is no agreed upon list of possible gender identifications that people might adopt. Nonetheless, some state and local governmental agencies have put into place legislation to protect citizens from discrimination based on their gender identification. Some governmental agencies recognize dozens of these. Such a stance might seem to emanate from some universe wholly unrelated to our local context, but institutions quite close to home, like public school systems and military bases, often grapple with this evolving consciousness. Educators across the country are increasingly sensitized to the challenges of gender discrimination, similar to decades-long training aimed at raising our awareness about racial or ethnic discrimination. This attentiveness is not simply a tactic to avoid disciplinary action against teachers or lawsuits against school districts. Rather, it goes to the very heart of the educational mission to nurture every student to achieve their full potential.

Preaching in the Midst of a New Reality

At the turn of the millennium, noted sociologist Zygmunt Bauman authored a prophetic work titled *Liquid Modernity*. Bauman argued that societies previously lived in a world of "solids," symbolized by manufacturing plants that employed you for a lifetime, stable governments that rendered reliable services, and trustworthy religious institutions that served as unerring moral beacons. The new millennium, however, was witnessing a different phenomenon. Stable financial systems were collapsing, social structures like the family were reconfiguring, traditional presuppositions about male and female roles were shattered, and a country like the United States that professed to be "one nation under God" was increasingly divided politically and religiously.

Refrain from "Them-ing"

There are two fundamental skills that are useful for preachers to cultivate when preaching in the midst of this new reality. The first is to avoid facile binaries when referencing people who appear to be wholly different than we are. Preachers need to be self-reflective enough to refrain from explicit or even implicit them-ing. Our homilizing can subtly enable them-ing through an ingrained inability to recognize any other country, religion, or political stance as beneficial to our own spiritual journey or evangelizing mission. This is the opposite of Pope Francis' affirmation that those who do not profess any religion are precious allies with the Roman Catholic in the struggle for human dignity. What the Pope demonstrates here is what the Swedish theologian and bishop Krister Stendahl called "holy envy." Through his own experience in interfaith dialogue, Stendahl developed three rules for religious understanding:

> 1) Let the other define herself (don't think you know the other without listening); 2) compare equal to equal (not my positive qualities to the negative ones of the other); and 3) find beauty in the other so as to develop "holy envy." (Landau 2007, 30)

These principles are helpful to those who wish to develop as detectives of divinity in the spirit of Barbara Brown Taylor.

If we do not know how to profess holy envy for those who identify with the LGBTQ (Lesbian, Gay, Bisexual, Transgender, and Questioning/

Queer) community, we must search for pathfinders to show us the way. Trusted mentors James and Evelyn Whitehead tackle this issue with typical style and grace. Specifically addressing the presence of transgender members of our families and faith communities, they chart out a path from bewilderment to celebrating God's extravagance. Witnessing someone discern their gender identity can be bewildering, potentially calling into question our previously constructed vision of personhood. This is not necessarily a bad thing, the Whiteheads advise. They note that "bewilderment stands as a portal to humility," and refer us to the multiple biblical narratives about those who have lost their secure path and find themselves launched into an unexpected spiritual journey (Whitehead and Whitehead 2014, 172). Moving through this humbling portal is an invitation to awe and praise for that signature feature of creation: God's extravagance. They write:

> We inhabit a universe that dazzles with its size and diversities. Astronomers inform us of the unthinkable enormity of multiple galaxies and innumerable black holes. The Director of the Vatican Observatory has noted that there are 10^{22} stars in the universe (this abbreviation signifies the number 10 followed by 22 zeroes). Such outsized numbers tax our comprehension. . . . Biologists tell us of the myriad forms of life that populate our own world even now; for example, 200 species of ants have been identified. How to explain this abundance? . . . The lavishness of creation assaults our minds and challenges our comprehension. A boundless generosity is on exhibit throughout our world. . . . The life experience of transgender persons also draws us into this story of God's extravagance." (173–174)

One reoccurring Easter Gospel that moves me to such holy envy is the tale of the two disciples on the road to Emmaus (Luke 24:13–35). While there are many intriguing elements in that pericope—for example, is the reason that one disciple is named (Cleopas) and the other is not because the latter was a woman, maybe Cleopas' wife?—most salient for me is Jesus' role as the stranger. This is a reversal for Jesus, who as a rule was cast in the role of the host, welcoming Samaritans, lepers, and other outcasts who had been estranged from Jewish society. Here, however, Jesus assumes the role of the unknown other who becomes an astonishing source of revelation. Ironically, if the holy stranger had not been welcomed by the two disciples, there would have been no possibility for Eucharist.

Speak Out in the Face of Discrimination and Violence

Besides nuancing our preaching to avoid them-ing and actually announce the grace and gift of others, the prophetic turn urges that preachers explicitly speak out when people experience discrimination and violence because of their ethnicity, race, sexual orientation, or gender. According to the most recent data from the Federal Bureau of Investigation, bias-motivated crimes against Jews and other religious minorities, black and Latinx citizens, and those in the LTBTQ community—especially transgender individuals—are on the rise. Unfortunately, we do not need to consult FBI statistics before addressing such bigotry in our preaching, since reports of blatant manifestations of such intolerance routinely flood local and national news. Stabbings of Orthodox Jews in New York celebrating Hanukah, the assault on a Sikh temple in Oak Creek, Wisconsin, the massacre at the Pulse nightclub in Orlando, Florida, and innumerable other hate crimes blight our national soul. The 1998 torture and murder of Matthew Shepard, who self-identified as gay, was so shocking that it prompted federal legislation in his name that classified as hate crimes those crimes motivated by the perception of someone's gender, sexual orientation, or disability.

Preachers are not problem solvers. We are not expected to use the pulpit as a platform for unraveling society's most puzzling dilemmas. At the same time, the mystifying nature of these inhumane acts is no excuse for playing the proverbial ostrich and burying our heads in the sand of the liturgy. Our mission, rather, is to name the evil and then to announce the hope that springs from Jesus' pivotal commandments of love. When I am dumbfounded by societal violence or ecclesial abuse, I confess my bafflement. More than that, however, I need to do the reflective work to discover where God's extravagant mercy emerges from such bewilderment, and where glimmers of resurrection appear in the midst of this fresh crucifixion. Brazilian archbishop and theologian Hélder

Câmara (d. 1999) is said to have remarked, "The darker the night, the more beautiful the dawn." How does our public theologizing as preachers both accompany local communities and prod our national conscience to make that difficult journey to dawn with integrity and empathy?

Conclusion

Mass Appeal is a celebrated two-character play featuring a complacent Roman Catholic pastor and his idealistic young transitional deacon. The pastor, Father Farley, is charming and quite popular with his affluent parishioners, who appreciate his entertaining but somewhat vapid preaching. The firebrand deacon, Mark Dolson, shuns the pastor's "song and dance theology" and wants to shake things up from the pulpit. Mark's approach is so confrontational, however, that what he considers prophetic others perceive as condemnatory. Over the course of the play both men change. Toward the end, the pastor, who cares deeply for Mark, tries to coach him as he prepares for a climactic preaching moment. The pastor tries to convince Mark that the challenge is not to get the people to like him, but the reverse: for Mark to express his care and love for the people. While exploring his ability to love, Mark talks about his beautiful tropical fish that died because someone turned up the heat in the tank. After reflecting on that experience, Mark ascends the pulpit one last time, relates the story of his fish, and regrets the fact that in that instance he did not have the kind of ears that could hear the screams of fish. He

> I had a tank of tropical fish. Someone turned up the tank heater and they all boiled. I . . . went to feed them and . . . all of my beautiful fish were floating on the top. . . . It looked like violence, but it was such a quiet night. And I remember wishing I had the kind of ears that could hear fish screams because they looked as if they suffered and I wanted so badly to save them. That Sunday in church, I heard that Christ told his apostles to be fishers of men. From then on, I looked at all the people in the church as fish. I was young so I saw them as beautiful tropical fish and so I knew that they were all quiet screamers. . . . I wanted the kind of ears that could hear what they were screaming about. . . . So now I'm back—listening—listening for the screams of angels."
>
> *Mass Appeal*, 63–64

expressed his hope that as a minister, as a preacher, he would learn to listen more intently, even for the "screams of angels."

Having ears to hear the silent cries of God's people—the joys of the newly engaged and the laments of the grieving, the questioning of the young and the bewilderment of the middle aged—is both a grace and a goal. As a holy gift and a human endeavor, it is never perfectly embraced or consistently practiced. However, that does not deter us from trying to develop ears to hear and eyes to see, and especially the capacity to empathize deeply with those who do not believe their cries are heard by the Church, or even by God. With humility and faith, we announce as St. Francis did at the end of his life, "Let us begin again, for up till now we have done so little."

References

The Center for Applied Research in the Apostolate online at https://cara .georgetown.edu/.

Chabris, Christopher and Daniel Simons. 2010. *The Invisible Gorilla: And Other Ways Our Intuitions Deceive Us.* New York: Crown Publishing.

Coates, Ta-Nehisi. 2015. *Between the World and Me.* New York: Spiegel and Grau.

D'Antonio, William D. 2011. "New Survey Offers Portrait of U.S. Catholics." *National Catholic Reporter,* https://www.ncronline.org/news/new-survey-offers -portrait-us-catholics

Davis, Bill. 2002. *Mass Appeal.* Rev. ed. New York: Dramatists Play Service.

Diamond, Milton. 2005. "Sex, Gender, and Identity over the Years: A Changing Perspective." *Child and Adolescent Psychiatric Clinics of North America* 13: 591–607.

Pope Francis. *Christus vivit (Chirst Is Alive).* 2019. http://www.vatican.va/content /francesco/en/apost_exhortations/documents/papa-francesco_esortazione-ap _20190325_christus-vivit.html.

Isasi-Díaz, Ada María and Yolanda Tarango. 1988. *Hispanic Women: Prophetic Voice in the Church.* New York: Harper and Row.

Jackson, Wes. 2005. "Toward an Ignorance-Based World View." *The Land Report* 81: 14–16. https://landinstitute.org/learn/land-report/.

Landau, Yehezkel. 2007. "An Interview with Krister Stendahl." *Harvard Divinity Bulletin* 35: 29–31.

Moschella, Mary Clark. 2008. *Ethnography as Pastoral Practice: An Introduction.* Cleveland: Pilgrim Press.

Norris, Kathleen. 1998. *The Quotidian Mysteries: Laundry, Liturgy and "Woman's Work."* New York: Paulist Press.

Pew Research Center: Religion and Public Life. Online at https://www.pewforum.org/.

Ryder, Norman B. 1965. "The Cohort as a Concept in the Study of Social Change." *American Sociological Review* 30, no. 6: 843–861.

Sapolsky, Robert. 2017. "Why Your Brain Hates Other People, and How to Make It Think Differently." *Nautilus* 55. https://medium.com/nautilus-magazine/why-your -brain-hates-other-people-35fb89809350.

Synod of Bishops. 2018. "Young People, the Faith and Vocational Discernment: *Instrumentum Laboris*." http://www.vatican.va/roman_curia/synod/documents/rc _synod_doc_20180508_instrumentum-xvassemblea-giovani_en.html.

Taylor, Barbara Brown. 2009. *Altars in the World: A Geography of Faith*. New York: Harper Collins.

———. 1999. *Home by Another* Way. Lanham, MD: Rowman and Littlefield.

Ward, Pete, ed. 2012. *Perspectives in Ecclesiology and Ethnography*. Grand Rapids: Eerdmans.

Whitehead, James D. and Evelyn E. Whitehead. 2014. *Fruitful Embraces: Sexuality, Love, and Justice*. Bloomingtion, IN: iUniverse.

CHAPTER

3

The Liturgies of the Church and the World

Attention, taken to its highest degree,
is the same thing as prayer.
It presumes faith and love.
Absolutely unmixed attention is prayer.

~Simone Weil

In the annals of twentieth-century rhetoric, few politicians have syn-thesized the mood of a country more effectively than Franklin Delano Roosevelt. In his address to a joint session of Congress and the nation the day after the surprise attack on Pearl Harbor, Roosevelt branded December 7, 1941, as "a date which will live in infamy." While the ensu-ing decades have witnessed the thaw and eventual thriving of cultural, economic, and even military ties between Japan and the United States, Roosevelt's words still echo in our national memory. One wonders what kind of preaching filled the pulpits of Roman Catholic churches on the following Sunday, December 14, 1941. There is virtually no documenta-tion of any.

A more recent day of infamy for US citizens was September 11, 2001 (9/11), when terrorists hijacked commercial airliners and attacked the twin towers of New York's World Trade Center and the Pentagon; a planned third assault by an airplane was scuttled by the passengers and crashed in rural western Pennsylvania. Political rhetoric, seldom as eloquent as Roosevelt's, filled the airwaves over the ensuing days and months. The victims of the attack were remembered at Masses during the next weeks, universally mentioned in the prayer of the faithful. There is anecdotal information, however, that many Roman Catholic clergy did not directly preach about the event in their Sunday homilies on September 16, 2001. In a notable discussion on the topic published in the Jesuit weekly review *America*, one permanent deacon tried to explain why this day of infamy never made it into so many pulpits. Responding to a previously published article on the topic in the same journal, he noted in his letter to the editor:

> Our training is at least partially responsible for our good and bad performance. It is so ingrained in me to preach from the [scriptural] text and only from the text that I rarely consider the possibility of doing something else. I think that this very fundamental insistence rooted in our homiletics training is responsible for helping to gradually raise the quality of preaching in our Catholic parishes, but it comes at the cost of reducing our ease in responding to external events and other situations. (Barbernitz 2002, 37–38)

This startling assessment honestly reflects the bind that many Roman Catholic preachers experience when addressing world events or social movements in the confines of Sunday Mass with its prescribed readings and texts. Can we, or do we, sermonize on the themes of Mother's Day when that date inevitably occurs on a Sunday of Easter or even on Pentecost? How do we construct a homily when the fourth of July falls on a Sunday? What do we say on those extended weekends celebrating national holidays like Martin Luther King Jr.'s birthday, Memorial Day, or Labor Day? One savvy preacher wisely advised a young colleague: "Issues reach the pulpit before you do." Sometimes, however, those issues hover there like some invisible gorilla, too problematic or perilous to name publicly.

When facing this quandary, I find helpful the insight of the Jesuit theologian Karl Rahner, who served as one of the theological experts for the German bishops during the Second Vatican Council. A theological optimist, Rahner was convinced that the universe is permeated by God's grace from its innermost roots. This idea was poetically announced by another famed Jesuit a century earlier, the poet Gerard Manley Hopkins, who penned the memorable line "The earth is charged with the grandeur of God." Because Rahner and many theologians like him believed that God has been self-communicating holy compassion to the world throughout our cosmic history, Rahner developed the concept of the "liturgy of the world." Liturgy in this sense existed before the worship of Christianity or even Judaism. Rahner understands this broader liturgical frame not as a set of texts or rubrics but as the reverent attending to God's abiding presence in the ordinary events and people that punctuate our lives. Akin to the previously referenced ideas of Barbara Brown Taylor, this foundational form of liturgy is an invitation to all humanity to pay attention to the mystery of life in all of its graces and tragedies as reflective of God's eternally attending to us.

In unpacking this concept, Rahner scholar Michael Skelley underscores how this liturgy of the world does not diminish the official liturgy of the Church but actually requires it. He explains that since God's self-revelation often lies unnoticed and concealed within the ordinary events of our lives, it is regularly overlooked. In order to open our eyes to this liturgy of God's continuous self-revelation in the great and small moments of life, we require the liturgies of the Church, especially the Eucharist. These official and public forms of worship are critical gifts for recalibrating our hearts to the depth of meaning embedded in our own existence and the baptismal vocation we are called to live out each day in the world (Skelley 1991, 94).

> This liturgy of the world is, as it were, veiled to the darkened eyes and the dulled heart of [people] which fails to understand its own true nature. This liturgy, therefore must . . . be interpreted, "reflected upon" in its ultimate depths in the celebration of that which we are accustomed to call liturgy in the more usual sense.
>
> Rahner 1983, 146

Analogously, it is enlightening to ponder the great and small moments of life in this broader liturgical frame. The tragedy of 9/11 was its own form of crucifixion. On the other hand, Mother's Day displays the human need for annunciations of whatever forms of new life grace our own families. Then there are those Independence Day celebrations and annual memorials of beloved war dead that attest to the violence of human history and the liberating freedom of the children of God. Each local festival of ethnic pride or international commemoration such as that recalling the genocide of European Jews during World War II is not an event to be ignored by Eucharistic worship and its preaching. Rather, this is the stuff of the liturgy of the world to be interpreted thoughtfully and publicly in the liturgies of the Church for the sake of the baptized and for the well-being of human society.

In Jesus' aforementioned encounter with the two disciples on the road to Emmaus (Luke 24:13–35), Jesus does not begin his revelation to these discouraged followers by immediately turning to Scripture. Rather, he inquires about what is weighing on their minds. Only after hearing their story of loss and wonderment does he turn to the Law and the Prophets. This is a powerful testimony about the revelatory potential of the liturgy of the world, recently played out for that distraught twosome on Golgotha, then in reports of an empty tomb, and in Jerusalem. Equally important is the way this passage manifests the need for critical reflection on such events in order to help the lost redirect their discipleship back on the right path to the risen Lord.

The Myth of Preaching *Sola Scriptura*

The comments of the permanent deacon cited above point to a widespread misunderstanding of Roman Catholic teaching about the homily. During the sixteenth-century Protestant Reformation, there was a strong insistence among many reformers about the primacy of Scripture in teaching and preaching. That emphasis was capsulized in the maxim "sola scriptura," Latin for "by Scripture alone." The theologizing behind this adage is that Sacred Scripture rather than any other source, such as Church tradition, is the essential litmus test for discerning authentic Christian teaching and practice. This scriptural turn also governed preaching within emerging Protestant churches. To this day, many of my Protestant colleagues hold that the Sunday sermon should only and essentially be grounded in a scriptural text: either chosen by the preacher or prescribed in the *Revised Common Lectionary*.

This renewed appreciation for the centrality of Scripture in teaching and preaching was a necessary corrective and contributed mightily to a more authentic view of our shared catholicity. The Second Vatican Council clearly embraced this emphasis. Its decrees are heavily accented with scriptural references. The *Dogmatic Constitution on Divine Revela-*

tion magisterially asserts that, together with sacred tradition, Scripture is the "supreme rule of faith" (21). It further notes that with sacred tradition it is the primary and perpetual foundation of theology (24). Regarding preaching, the *Constitution on Divine Revelation* teaches that Scripture must nourish and regulate all the preaching of the Church (21).

Unfortunately, however, this essential turn to Scripture in preaching has been too narrowly understood and even misunderstood by many. The already mentioned *Fulfilled in Your Hearing,* issued by the United States Bishops' Committee on Priestly Life and Ministry in 1982, quickly became a key text for shaping future preachers in Roman Catholic seminaries, diaconal formation, and other training programs. While there is much to applaud about this ground-breaking document, it regrettably offers a limited view of the sources for the homily, which it frames almost exclusively in terms of the scriptural proclamation that precedes it. Thus, *Fulfilled in Your Hearing* defines the homily as "scriptural interpretation of human existence" (82) and instructs that "a homily flows out of the Scriptures of the Liturgy of the Word" (100). This appears to be the very constriction that our permanent deacon admits in his above-cited letter to the editor. *Fulfilled in Your Hearing* was replaced in 2012 by another document from the United States Conference of Catholic Bishops, *Preaching the Mystery of Faith.* While this replacement document gives more attention to the liturgical context than does *Fulfilled in Your Hearing,* it yet contends that the lectionary readings are the "prime basis" for the homily, although illustrations from other texts of the Eucharistic liturgy are allowed (18).

The Church's most significant teaching on this matter continues to be the Second Vatican Council's *Constitution on the Sacred Liturgy.* In a pivotal passage, this document notes, "By means of the homily, the mysteries of the faith and the guiding principles of the Christian life are expounded from the sacred text during the course of the liturgical year" (52). While many are inclined to consider "sacred text" a synonym for "Scripture" or "lectionary text" the Vatican does not. The year after the promulgation of this document, the Vatican released its first official interpretation of various aspects of it, including a definitive explanation of the phrase "sacred text."

A homily on the sacred text means an explanation, pertinent to the mystery celebrated and the special needs of the listeners, of some point in **either** the readings from sacred Scripture or in another text from the Ordinary **or** Prayer of the day's Mass. (*Inter Oecumenici*, 54, emphasis added)

Notice the reoccurring word *or* in this passage. This unambiguous interpretation—repeated in the *Code of Canon Law* (c. 767 §1)—makes it clear that authentic liturgical preaching for Roman Catholics does not necessitate always preaching explicitly from the Scriptures. In their 2003 *Introduction to the Order of Mass*, the United States Catholic bishops go even further, noting: "By means of the homily the mysteries of the faith and the guiding principles of Christian living are expounded, most often from the Scriptures proclaimed but also from the other texts *and rites* of the liturgy" (92, emphasis added). This is a well-balanced statement that recognizes the centrality of the scriptural texts for preaching, but also acknowledges the flexibility preachers have in the shadow of some new "day of infamy" or other contemporary event. Maybe if our diaconal brother and others recognized this freedom—even though the scriptural texts of the day might not have provided a homiletic opening—some other liturgical resource, such as the second Eucharistic Prayer for Reconciliation, may have offered a path for homilizing in the wake of 9/11. Who knows what effect praying and preaching such a prayer across the country might have had in the aftermath of this tragic event and others like it.

> In the midst of conflict and division, we know it is you who turn our minds to thoughts of peace. Your Spirit changes our hearts: enemies begin to speak to one another, those who were estranged join hands in friendship, and nations seek the way of peace together.
>
> Your Spirit is at work when understanding puts an end to strife, when hatred is quenched by mercy, and vengeance gives way to forgiveness.
>
> Excerpt from Eucharistic Prayer for Reconciliation II, *Sacramentary*, 1975, in use at the time of 9/11

Feeding the Catholic Imagination

One of the more colorful national Catholic figures in recent memory was priest, sociologist, novelist, professor, and irrepressible commentator Andrew Greeley. Over his lifetime, he published seventy-two works of nonfiction and sixty-six novels, in addition to innumerable articles, columns, interviews, and sermons. It was often suggested that Greeley never had an unpublished thought, an idea he acknowledged and never refuted. While his thinking traversed fields of politics, feminism, education, and his own Irish heritage, over time Greeley developed a special focus on what he came to call the Catholic imagination. This concept was grounded in the work of theologian David Tracy, his friend and colleague at the University of Chicago.

In early 1981, Tracy published his mind-expanding classic titled *The Analogical Imagination: Christian Theology and the Culture of Pluralism*. One of the key insights in this work is Tracy's contention that a Catholic imagination is one that perceives the world in all of its variety as a sacrament (413). While the world does not reveal or deplete the whole of the mystery of God, it is more similar to than different from the Holy One. What Tracy calls an "analogical imagination" Mary Catherine Hilkert calls a "sacramental imagination." Like Tracy and Rahner, Hilkert affirms that a dominant strand of thinking evident throughout centuries of Roman Catholic theology and practice is a belief in the positive and graced nature of the world. Consequently, she speaks about preaching as "the art of naming grace" (44).

Over the years, Greeley came to embrace this characterization of a Catholic imagination as a sacramental one, but thought that as a social scientist he could empirically prove that it actually existed. Some of his published research considered how the Catholic imagination played out in public arenas. Thus, for example, he could demonstrate that Roman Catholics show more preference for the fine arts than the national average and even our Protestant counterparts (Greeley 1996). Other investigations focused specifically on explicit liturgical and sacramental practices of Roman Catholics. In one striking study conducted in the Archdiocese of Chicago, the research focused on why people wanted to be or remain Catholic. Greeley's conclusion was that people stay Roman

Catholic because of the sacraments, which he labels "uniquely Catholic" (Greeley 1991, 12–13). Greeley eventually came to believe that Roman Catholics not only have a sacramental imagination but, indeed, a "liturgical imagination."

Admittedly, much has happened within the Catholic Church and the United States since Greeley's initial research. Nonetheless, according to various surveys, studies, and interviews—including some from the Center for Applied Research in the Apostolate—the role of sacramentality continues to loom large in the Catholic imagination. Despite the exit of many from the Roman Catholic Church over the past few decades, sacraments and sacramentals are still spiritually potent. Consider all of the disaffiliated or intermittent Mass attenders who yet show up for ashes at the outset of Lent, want their babies baptized, cannot imagine getting married in anything but a "Catholic" church, and summon the priest for the necessary rituals in the face of impending death.

> Catholics live in an enchanted world, a world of statues and holy water, stained glass and votive candles, saints and religious medals, rosary beads and holy pictures. But these Catholic paraphernalia are mere hints of a deeper and more pervasive religious sensibility which inclines Catholics to see the Holy lurking in creation.
>
> Greeley,
> The Catholic Imagination, 1

The reason I take this sacramental excursion in the midst of pondering homilizing within worship is to accentuate the need for preaching the whole of the sacramental liturgy and life of the Church. Despite the critical turn to Scripture in Church teaching and liturgical theology since Vatican II, Roman Catholics generally do not have a scriptural imagination. In my experience, most Catholics consistently seem more adept at recalling lyrics from their favorite liturgical music—be that "Holy God, We Praise Thy Name" or "On Eagle's Wings"—than texts from the lectionary. Homilists have a responsibility to nurture a deep love of God's Word in our assemblies and ignite that scriptural imagination that is clearly more prevalent among many Protestants. However, this needs to be paired with an appreciation of the sacramental imagination that flows in abundance through our lived catholicity and needs to be respected in our preaching.

Preaching about sacramental actions has a distinguished and ancient pedigree. One of the most stirring comes from St. Augustine of Hippo, arguably the Western Church's most influential theologian. In the early fifth century, he preached a Pentecost sermon to those initiated at Easter just weeks before. In that homily he famously invokes multiple gestures, texts, and actions from rituals that these newly initiated recently experienced to drive home the significance of the Eucharist that they are about to receive again. While Augustine cites two verses from St. Paul, he spends most of the homily exegeting the actions that surrounded the entry of these newborn believers into the Church: the placing of bread on the table and in their hands, their "Amen" response at communion, rituals of exorcism, baptismal plungings, and the confirming gift of the Holy Spirit. Augustine was preaching to the whole Christian: mind, heart, and body. He was homilizing on the theologies inscribed on their physical selves, the incarnate souls that were plunged into water, slathered with chrism, and fed with Christ's Body and Blood. These are the same bodies that are commissioned to witness Christ's presence in the world, sacramental instruments of a fully sacramental imagination.

Today we preach to similarly embodied baptized. While many of them have not traveled through the full sensory experience of adult

> So now if you want to understand the body of Christ, listen to the Apostle Paul speaking to the faithful: You are the body of Christ, member for member. If you, therefore, are Christ's body and members, it is your own mystery that is placed on the Lord's table! It is your own mystery that you are receiving! You are saying Amen to what you are—your response is a personal signature, affirming your faith. When you hear "The Body of Christ," you reply, "Amen." Be a member of Christ's body, then, so that your Amen may ring true!
>
> But what role does the bread play? We have no theory of our own to propose here; listen, instead, to what Paul says about this sacrament: The bread is one, and we, though many, are one body. Understand and rejoice— unity, truth, faithfulness, love. One bread, he says. What is this one bread? Is it not the one body, formed from many? Remember: bread doesn't come from a single grain but from many. When you received exorcism, you were ground. When you were baptized, you were leavened. When you received the fire of the Holy Spirit, you were baked. Be what you see; receive what you are.
>
> Augustine, Sermon 272

initiation, they consistently use their bodies in worship to sign themselves, to kneel, to beat their breasts, to offer peace, and to extend their hands for receiving Communion. These are symbols of incipient theologies deeply embedded in Christians' flesh and waiting for our exegesis. A few years ago, when preparing to preach about the radical hospitality of Jesus in his welcoming of Zacchaeus (Luke 19:1–10), I nonchalantly glanced at the crucifix in my room. It struck me that Jesus was nailed on the cross in an eternal gesture of hospitality. His arms could never close, because the Sacred Heart of God had no capacity for doing so. It is the same gesture many people make while praying the Our Father. At each Eucharist we do not physically pantomime some ancient gesture whose meaning seems lost to the ages, but inhabit a corporal symbol whose body language is understood across cultures. When we pray the Lord's Prayer we do not cross our arms or fold our hands, but we open our whole selves in a vulnerable stance of hospitality. Mirroring the woundedness of the crucified, we repeatedly inscribe on our bodies his mission to be vulnerable as we collaborate in bringing about the reign of God's justice and peace to a sometimes-unwelcoming world. He opened wide his arms in welcoming Zacchaeus. We do the same.

The Lectionary and Holy Billiards

In the classic musical *The Music Man*, the loveable huckster Harold Hill begins his public swindle of the folk of River City, Iowa, with a showstopping musical tirade against the game of pool. "Ya got trouble," the self-styled "Professor" Hill warns parents, while extolling billiards as the superior game. While I am neither a pool prohibitionist nor advocate, when it comes to lectionary preaching, I prefer billiards and the corresponding wisdom it offers.

The object of the game of pool—also known as pocket billiards— is to sink the balls in one of the six pockets around the table's edges. The game of eight ball specifically requires players to call their shots, announcing which ball—either a solid-colored ball (numbered 1 through 7) or a striped one (9 through 15)—they intend to sink in which pocket, then finally sinking the black eight ball to win. In contrast, carom, or French billiards, is played on a table with no pockets and only three balls, ordinarily two white and one red. One scores points in this game

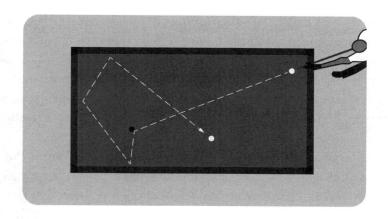

not by pocketing any balls, but by driving a white ball into the other two balls in a single stroke. This game requires the ability to calculate vectors in order to achieve the hoped-for ricochet. This task is rendered even more complex in three-cushion billiards, in which the cue ball strikes one other ball and then three or more cushions before striking the second object ball. One wonders whether you need an advanced degree in Euclidian geometry or even calculus in order to be successful in this sport.

While crafting a homily rooted in the lectionary is not exactly playing billiards with God, it does require some homiletic calculus that can position the readings of the day so that they can metaphorically ricochet off one other for a more abundant unfolding of God's Word. Roman Catholics have had over a half century to become familiar with the structure of the reformed lectionary mandated by Vatican II. On a typical Sunday, we are given a Gospel from the designated synoptic writer for that liturgical year (e.g., Matthew for Year A), a first reading ordinarily chosen to harmonize with that Gospel, and a semi-continuous second reading that often has little to do with the narratives or themes of the other two readings. Then, of course, there is the psalm. While the responsorial psalm is most often considered a response to God's Word, this somewhat misleading title does not diminish the fact that the psalm is also God's Word and thus an integral part of the scriptural assets that equip us for preaching.

One of the unusual aspects of the current lectionary that sometimes complicates our engagement in this holy billiards is the way that the scriptural texts have been edited for use at Mass. With some regularity, the lectionary texts have been trimmed to eliminate or make optional particular verses and even large sections of a chapter. This is almost always the case with the responsorial psalm and frequently occurs with the first reading in order to align it more closely with the Gospel. Not surprisingly, this approach has received much criticism. Some have crafted their own lectionaries as a corrective.

Our task as preachers in the Roman Catholic tradition is not to create our own lectionary or redesign the Roman Missal. These gifts to the universal Church have largely achieved one key reforming goal of Vatican II: to open up more lavishly the treasures of the Bible and provide God's people a "richer fare . . . at the table of God's Word" (*Constitution on the Sacred Liturgy*, 51). These resources call preachers to develop interpretative approaches to the lectionary that are related but not identical to the skills of biblical exegesis we may have learned in school. Scripture scholar Dianne Bergant explains this development at the beginning of the three-volume commentary on the lectionary she authored with liturgist Richard Fragomeni. Bergant writes:

> The Lectionary, while not identical to the Bible, is drawn from its contents, providing a kind of narrative infrastructure for celebration of the Liturgical Year. The Lectionary is drawn from sacred Scripture by selecting passages from the biblical material (decontextualizing) and then places these readings within a new literary and liturgical context (recontextualizing), thus creating a new ecclesial genre. This recontextualization of former biblical material calls for a new way of interpretation, one that takes into consideration the liturgical character and setting of the Lectionary readings. (Bergant and Fragomeni 2001, vii)

Bergant recognizes that a key interpretive lens for excavating the lectionary readings is the very structure of worship itself, especially the liturgical year with its rhythm of seasons and feasts. Another specialist on the subject, Fritz West, declares this to be "the Catholic principle" that actually drives the strategy behind the design of the Roman Catholic lectionary. This principle recognizes that in our tradition Scripture is not only interpreted *through* the liturgy, but that the biblical texts are fundamentally shaped and even selected *because of* the cycle of feasts and seasons. In comparison, when scriptural texts are the driving elements for determining a season or celebration, West deems this the "Protestant principle" (West 1997, 47–52).

This Catholic principle is a persistent but often unrecognized bedrock of parochial worship. When planning a wedding, a funeral, or an ordination, we ordinarily do not start by considering the prescribed lections for the day, or presume that such will even be proclaimed. Rather, we begin with the people and ritual event at hand that position us to select texts appropriate to the liturgy and the anticipated gathered assembly. One of the more startling examples of this principle, embedded in the official *Rite of Christian Initiation of Adults*, demonstrates how our initiatory ceremonies shape the lectionary. Most liturgical leaders are aware that we can use the Year A Gospels in Years B and C on the Third, Fourth, and Fifth Sundays of Lent, since those lections are particularly suited to the scrutinies ordinarily occurring on those Sundays (*Lectionary for Mass: Introduction*, 97). Many would be surprised to learn that, even outside Lent—if and when the elect are undergoing scrutinies in the process of full initiation—those same three Lenten Gospels are not only allowed but actually mandated as part of the ritual Masses for the scrutinies (*Rite of Christian Initiation of Adults*, 146). Consequently, if for good pastoral reasons, your parish has chosen to baptize an adult on the Feast of Christ the King, the Lenten Gospels from Year A are proclaimed in the scrutinies leading up to that initiation on the preceding Sundays or even weekdays. The feast sets the readings and thus becomes a critical interpretive frame for preaching those readings.

When most of us studied Scripture, we learned various styles of exegesis and hermeneutical approaches; we seldom exercised those skills through any liturgical lens or even considered the seasonal context in the process. That usually had to wait until the preaching classes. If all preaching must be contextual, however, the liturgical context of the lectionary and its powerful interpretive optics cannot be an afterthought. This realization is not an invitation to abandon historical-critical methods, badmouth redaction criticism, or develop a careless disregard for serious analysis of the lectionary texts. It does require, however, that we deploy such skills in a liturgical mode. Doing so validates in a particular way that our homilizing is authentically Roman Catholic and truly liturgical.

The Sacred Texts and Ceremonial Time

While the term *cult classic* might call to mind a film such as *The Rocky Horror Picture Show* or one of the many *Godzilla* movies, it is an apt label for John Hanson Mitchell's quirky yet poetic book *Ceremonial Time*. Subtitled *Fifteen Thousand Years on One Square Mile*, the author spends over two hundred pages musing on an unremarkable patch of countryside west of Boston, which Mitchell admits is "nowhere" yet "everywhere." The author's technique for uncovering the human and historical richness of this place, traditionally known as Scratch Flat, is through the lens of ceremonial time.

The concept of ceremonial time that underpins this writing comes from local Native Americans who served as Mitchell's informants and guides as he struggled to envision the legacy of this singular patch of land. Distinct from linear or chronological time, Mitchell learned from the indigenous elders that ceremonial time allows the past, present, and future to fuse so they can be realized together in the now. Mitchell comes to understand that this fusion most often occurs ceremonially, for example, through ritual dances. Such rituals are potent vehicles for shattering the boundaries of time and allow, for instance, the conjoining of a Paleolithic event with the present. Through this experience of ceremonial time-shifting, Mitchell learns not only how better to grasp a rich though previously unknown past, but also how to become one with it. Ultimately, Mitchell believes such

> Wilderness and wildlife, history, life itself, for that matter, is something that takes place somewhere else, it seems. You must travel to witness it, you must get in your car in summer and go off to look at things which some "expert," such as the National Park Service, tells you is important, or beautiful, or historic. In spite of their admitted grandeur, I find such well-documented places somewhat boring. What I prefer, and the thing that is the subject of this book, is that undiscovered country of the nearby, the secret world that lurks beyond the night windows and at the fringes of cultivated backyards.
>
> Mitchell, *Ceremonial Time*, 7

exercises for finding our way in the past are critical for more fully perceiving the "undiscovered country of the nearby."

There are multiple parallels between Mitchell's quest to know his own geographic backyard and the homilist's vocation to befriend the liturgical terrain that sets the spiritual geography for much of our life's preaching. While not exactly our ritual backyard, the texts and liturgical structures that we traverse each week—often with numbing regularity—are a kind of "undiscovered country of the nearby." While familiarity does not necessarily breed contempt, it is prone to breed inattention, as Santayana suggested. Some of us are called upon to preach and preside with such frequency that we no longer believe that we have the time, much less the energy, to delve seriously into the multitude of prayers and ritual particularities that constitute Sunday worship, as well as weekday worship. The vast majority of contemporary Roman Catholic preachers would never approach the pulpit without at least glancing at, if not seriously pondering, the prescribed lections for the day. In my experience, however, few presiders crack open the missal or other ritual book before an impending celebration. Too often, the first time a presider encounters the opening oration is when the book is opened for praying. It strikes me as at least ironic if not disappointing that a presider would take the liberty to proclaim a text that had not previously been selected, digested, and prayed through.

Mitchell's exploration of ceremonial time provides a compelling enticement for burrowing deep into the liturgical texts that lie within arm's reach of our everyday preaching and presiding. In probing the historical richness of Scratch Flats, Mitchell's indigenous guides demonstrated for him the potency of rituals for shattering linear time and allowing the merging of past, present, and future experiences to invite us into the cumulative wisdom of the ages. Similarly, Roman Catholic worship is constructed on the firm foundation of "memorial." The centrality of this remembering (in Greek, *anamnesis*) is so critical that in our Catholic tradition, remembering the death and resurrection of the Lord must form the nucleus of sacraments such as baptism and Eucharist for them to be valid.

The English word *memorial*, however, can be somewhat misleading because of its seeming accent on historical events as completed and forever sealed in the past. This is akin to our yearly recalling of the attack on Pearl Harbor, whose anniversary has virtually no impact on the lives of most citizens of the United States today. Even though my father served in the Navy during World War II, for me that anniversary evokes little more than a fond memory of visiting the Pearl Harbor memorial with him toward the end of his life. For Christians, however, the mystery of Christ's death and resurrection is not historically sealed in the past like some long-ago military battle. His death and resurrection are not merely a spiritual memory. Rather, we profess the bedrock belief that these events—the paschal mystery—proclaim in a singular way the very life of the Trinity. While uniquely revealed only once in human history, the cosmic love displayed in this dying and rising exists yet today and continues to animate the whole of our Christian existence. Our sacred rituals, like those of Mitchell's indigenous mentors, are privileged paths into this remembering and serve as graced portals into the mystery of the ever-present God revealed in Jesus Christ.

As a consequence, our liturgies are also an indispensable resource for preaching that is crafted to reinvigorate and sustain the mystery of Christ's dying and rising in the lives of believers. Our rituals are a treasure trove of actions and texts, gestures and songs that illuminate the invitation into the paschal mystery in rich and exceptional ways. Prefaces and Eucharistic Prayers, actions of breaking and giving, and the profusion of other orations and symbolic acts that constitute our liturgies, are at the core of the "sacred texts" around which Vatican II positions our homilizing. Unfortunately, they are also a largely undiscovered country in our worship and rarely integrated into our preaching.

Prefaces might be a good place to start in expanding our skills in this high-stake endeavor of "preaching billiards." For example, the fact that Advent has two distinctive prefaces—the first prescribed for use through December 16 and the second deployed after that date—is telling information about the particular nature of Advent and its preaching. Although it might be surprising for some, the first Advent preface makes no explicit mention of the nativity, and has a strong future trajectory. When that proper text interacts with the readings of the opening Sundays of Advent—which also have no focus on Jesus' nativity—it becomes clear that Advent is not the run up to Jesus' annual birthday party. Rather, it is a distinctive proclamation that the mystery of the Incarnation has a future. This liturgical ricochet then asks how we participate in the incarnation now and in the time to come, and suddenly Advent pivots: it is not simply about past events but actually about present and future mission.

In 1837, American philosopher and poet Ralph Waldo Emerson was invited to offer a lecture to the Harvard chapter of the Phi Beta Kappa Society in Cambridge, Massachusetts. In that presentation, Emerson broached the topic of creativity again and again, arguing that the ability to create is actually an indicator of divine presence. In that discourse, he proposed to his audience that they not only engage in creative writing but also in "creative reading." He comments:

> One must be an inventor to read well. . . . There is then creative reading as well as creative writing. When the mind is braced by labor and invention, the page of whatever book we read becomes luminous with manifold allusion. Every sentence is doubly significant, and the sense of our author is as broad as the world. (Emerson 1837)

In that same vein I would suggest that the liturgical context and the prayer and ritual resources of our liturgical books are essential catalysts for creatively reading the lectionary texts so crucial to our homilizing. Having immersed ourselves in the spirituality of a liturgical season, especially by acquainting ourselves with its distinctive prayers and ritual actions, we are uniquely positioned to draw upon the Catholic imagination of our hearers and fulfill our responsibility to preach the sacred texts.

Roman Missal: Recipe or Resource?

John Shea is a gifted storyteller and narrative theologian who has the rare ability to delight and provoke at the same time. A favorite story that carries this double punch is his apparently fictional account of a daughter keen on documenting the recipe for her mother's incomparable Irish soda bread. Like many of her generation, the mother has no written recipe; instead, she has memories, practices, and instincts. Multiple times the daughter tries to replicate this cultural heirloom, and while the final product is always deemed "good" by the family, it never matches the quality of her mother's. The mystical twist at the end of Shea's story is not only a spiritual testament to the very reason why bread is such a potent symbol of Jesus, but also a reminder that feeding people's hunger can never be reduced to a recipe.

When many of us were trained to preach and preside, we sometimes inherited explicit or more often implicit recipes for constructing a sermon or enacting worship. In the process, many came to believe that the Roman Missal and the Lectionary, like other ritual books, prescribe a series of inflexible formulas that must be followed in order for the worship to be proper and legal. What may be surprising—and perhaps a touch liberating—for those of us who announce these sacred texts is section 7 of the *General Instruction of the Roman Missal*, "The Choice of the Mass and Its Parts." The very title not only highlights the fact that there are textual choices to be made, but also subtly reminds those who

Sarah took copious notes. Each pinch and dab and sprinkle were scribbled on her yellow pad. . . . Sarah's mother began to make the bread, she seemed to go into a trance. She moved gracefully around the kitchen and her hands were as swift and precise as a concert pianist's. Sarah had all she could do to keep up. . . .

The next day Sarah taped her notes to the cabinet door and began meticulously to follow the instructions. . . . That night at dinner she presented the family with all the anxiety of a bride's first meal. Her family praised the soda bread extravagantly but unanimously agreed that it was not as good as grandma's. . . .

That made Sarah more determined than ever and sent her back for a second note-taking session. The next afternoon her mother began her ritual of baking. Everything was as Sarah had marked it down. She could not see where she had gone wrong. . . .

"Ma, I did everything just as you did, but it didn't turn out the same." "You forgot the yeast," her mother said. "You don't use yeast in soda bread," said Sarah. "You use yeast in everything," instructed her mother. "I didn't see you use it." [Her mother responded,] "When I was kneading the dough, I saw all the faces of all the people who would eat it. The yeast entered the dough and made it bread." "What are you?" Sarah asked, laughing, "some kind of bread mystic?" Her mother smiled, but she did not deny it.

John Shea, 1987

Preaching as Paying Attention: Theological Reflection in the Pulpit

lead prayer that choosing texts is a critical step in preachers' and presiders' preparations. One small sign that this preparatory step is taken seriously is that the missal sitting in the sacristy or on the side table in the sanctuary opens easily or lays flat on the page of any Eucharistic Prayer besides II. There are fourteen approved Eucharistic Prayers for use in the United States. Most assemblies would never know that. A number of years ago a colleague was reported to the local bishop by a group of seminarians for using an "illegal" Eucharistic Prayer. It was the second Eucharistic Prayer for Reconciliation; they had never heard it. As folk wisdom would have it: choosing not to choose is a choice. It is, in effect, to choose badly.

The opening sentence of section 7 of the *General Instruction of the Roman Missal* alerts us to the priority of local pastoral needs in this selection process:

> The pastoral effectiveness of a celebration will be greatly increased if the texts of the readings, the prayers, and the liturgical chants correspond as aptly as possible to the needs, the preparation, and the culture of the participants. This will be achieved by appropriate use of the many possibilities of choice described below. (352)

This pastoral preeminence is further echoed in the *Lectionary for Mass: Introduction,* which notes:

> The first concern of a priest celebrating with a congregation is the spiritual benefit of the faithful and he will be careful not to impose his personal preference on them. (83)

What choices do we have that can feed our preaching and better position us to provide "spiritual benefit" to the faithful? Eucharistic Prayers are certainly key here, as are those theologically potent prefaces. There is great latitude in selecting these. On weekdays when there are no proper orations assigned, the *General Instruction* further allows for the use of one of the many "Prayers for Various Needs" provided in the Missal (363). This option only works, however, if we have set aside time to study the Missal. In so doing, we might discover the incredible wealth of options and ideas that render this not a collection of recipes but a plentiful resource of traditions and theologies that multiplies the textual vectors in our "playing billiards" with God.

In periods of special duress, local authorities can also suggest and permit the use of these resources even on Sunday. The section "For Civil Needs" is especially ample; there are texts "For the Preservation of Peace and Justice," "In Time of War or Civil Disturbance," "For Refugees and Exiles," "In time of Earthquake," "For Rain," and "For an End to Storms," to name a few. Even if these texts are not proclaimed, they are yet an abundant resource for preachers who may not find appropriate resources in the lections to address the distressing liturgy of the world that confronts their communities at any given moment. Just as a homilist can quote effectively from a Scripture passage that was not prescribed for that day's liturgy, so we can exploit the riches of the Roman Missal in untold ways in our quest for authentic liturgical preaching.

Conclusion

The Anglican poet and priest Malcolm Guite has penned a series of discerning sonnets for the liturgical year. He introduces these useful homiletic resources with an ode to the lectern. He writes:

> Some rise on eagles' wings, this one is plain,
> Plain English workmanship in solid oak.
> Age gracefully it says, go with the grain.
> You walk towards an always open book,
> Open as every life to every light,
> Open to shade and shadow, day and night,
> The changeless witness of your changing pain.
> Be still the Lectern says, stand here and read.
> Here are your mysteries, your love and fear,
> And, running through them all, the slender thread
> Of God's strange grace, red as these ribbons, red
> As your own blood when reading reads you here
> And pierces joint and marrow . . . So you stand,
> The lectern still beneath your trembling hand. (Guite, 2)

Such wisdom does not spill forth from someone who is a mere observer of lecterns. Rather, its origin must be in the experience of one who has personally traversed that wholly terrifying path toward the open book. In those unsealed pages are the mysteries and mercies that we anticipate proclaiming but which, in turn, read us as well: piercing "joint and marrow" and plunging us deeply into paschal dying and rising. In this holy immersion our needs and weaknesses, our prayers and intentions are splayed open in the presence of a fiercely attentive God who renews the Gospel call to stay awake to these mysteries unfolding in our lives. This fresh awakening alerts us to the unnoticed threads of godly grace that weave through the liturgy of the world and crave illumination in the Church's official worship.

Guite's lectern is a powerful metaphor for that holy arena in which preachers dance and wrestle with godly revelation in lectionary and missal, pericope and prayer, song and ritual gesture. It is a formidable place, filled with challenges and promises of conversion for preacher and hearer alike. In the twelfth chapter of his *Confessions*, St. Augustine narrates the pivotal moment in his turning toward God, which was triggered by a voice of a child chanting over and over again *"tolle lege, tolle lege,"* Latin for "take up and read, take up and read." And so, the as yet unconverted saint took up Paul's Letter to the Romans, read the verse at 13:13—"Let us conduct ourselves properly as in the day, not in orgies and drunkenness, not in promiscuity and licentiousness, not in rivalry and jealousy"—experienced the consolation of God, and in his words "the gloom of doubt vanished." We are also called to take up and read the whole of the liturgy in world and worship, in sacred lives and sacred texts. The promise of conversion for all of us lies therein as well. For the homilist, though, there is a further critical imperative necessary for that turning to God. We take up, we read, but then we preach! *Tolle, lege, praedica!*

References

Augustine. Sermon 272. Translated by Nathan Mitchell. *Assembly* 23, no. 2 (1997): 14.

Barbernitz, Peter. 2002. "Letters to the Editor." *America* (February 4, 2002): 36–38.

Bergant, Dianne with Richard Fragomeni. 1999–2001. *Preaching the New Lectionary.* 3 Volumes: *Year A; Year B; Year C.* Collegeville, MN: Liturgical Press.

Emerson, Ralph Waldo. 1847. "The American Scholar." Address in Cambridge, Massachusetts. http://digitalemerson.wsulibs.wsu.edu/exhibits/show/text/the-american-scholar.

Greeley, Andrew. 2001. *The Catholic Imagination.* Berkeley: University of California Press.

———. 1996. "Catholics, Fine Arts and the Liturgical Imagination." *America* 174, no. 18: 9–12, 14.

———. 1991. "Sacraments Keep Catholics High on the Church." *National Catholic Reporter* (April 12, 1991): 12–13.

Guite, Malcolm. 2012. "The Lectern," from *Sounding the Seasons: Seventy Sonnets for the Christian Year.* Norwich: Canterbury Press.

Hilkert, Mary Catherine. 1997. *Name Grace: Preaching and the Sacramental Imagination.* New York: Continuum.

Rahner, Karl. 1983. "On the Theology of Worship." *Theological Investigations.* Vol. 19. New York: Crossroad.

Shea, John. 1987. *The Spirit Master.* Chicago: Thomas More Press.

Skelley, Michael. 1991. *The Liturgy of the World: Karl Rahner's Theology of Worship.* Collegeville, MN: Liturgical Press.

Tracy, David. 1981. *The Analogical Imagination.* New York: Crossroad.

West, Fritz. 1997. *Scripture and Memory: The Ecumenical Hermeneutic of the Three-Year Lectionaries.* Collegeville, MN: Liturgical Press.

Weil, Simone. 2002. *Gravity and Grace.* Trans. Emma Crawford and Mario von der Ruhr. London: Rutledge, 117.

CHAPTER
4

Reversing the Galileo Effect

The world is but a canvas to our imagination.

~Henry David Thoreau

E pur si mouve. According to a widely circulated legend, those were the words that Galileo Galilei muttered under his breath as he left his trial before the court of the Roman Inquisition in 1633. The Italian phrase *e pur si mouve* roughly translates as "nevertheless, it does move." It is a pointed reference to a then controversial scientific position about the structure of the universe. For decades Galileo had been challenged by theologians and Church officials for his belief in heliocentrism: a theory proposing that the earth revolves around the sun (*helios* in Greek). Dating back to the ancient Greeks, this theory found fresh support through the work of the Renaissance mathematician Nicolaus Copernicus (d. 1543). Even though Copernicus was a Roman Catholic cleric and held a doctorate in canon law, his work was condemned after his death because it was considered incompatible with the biblical revelation and common Catholic belief. Among other scriptural texts, Psalm 93:1 was often used to refute this theory: "The world will surely stand in place, never to be moved."

Galileo's astronomical observations led him to affirm Copernicus' theory, although at the time there was no scientific experiment capable of proving it objectively. Such an experiment would only appear two centuries later. As early as 1613, voices were raised in opposition to Galileo's support of heliocentrism, and a few years later he was required to travel to Rome and defend his views. Eventually a commission of the Inquisition condemned heliocentrism as heretical, and Galileo was

71

instructed to abandon his belief in it. Over the decades, with changes in Church leadership and even papal backing, Galileo was encouraged to continue work around this issue, and in 1632 he wrote his definitive work on the topic. The publication of his *Dialogue Concerning the Two Chief World Systems,* however, ignited a firestorm of protest and the evaporation of papal support. Summoned before the Inquisition again, he was eventually found "vehemently suspect of heresy." His *Dialogue* was banned, publication of future works was prohibited, and Galileo spent the rest of his life under house arrest. Despite the condemnation and confinement, Galileo was yet unwavering in his belief in heliocentrism. *E pur si mouve!*

Almost 350 years later, in 1992, Pope St. John Paul II officially declared that Galileo was right. His *Dialogue* and the writings of Copernicus already had been removed from the Index of Forbidden Books in the nineteenth century. However, it was not until the late twentieth century that a committee from the Pontifical Academy finally concluded that, while the Inquisition had acted in good faith, it was ultimately wrong. Galileo's tenacity as well as his well-reasoned arguments seem finally to have paid off.

Physicist Jaroslav Hynecek describes the "Galileo effect" as a persistent belief—whether occurring in the fields of sociology, economics, religion, or even a hard science like physics—that endures despite the fact that there is no evidence for that belief or even clear evidence to the contrary. Hynecek employs this lens to demonstrate that Albert Einstein's celebrated general relativity theory is not only flawed but is the wrong framework for thinking about gravity. While I am in no position to judge whether his critique of Einstein is valid, I am empathetic to his broader conclusion. In the end, Hynecek asserts that the enduring blindness around this famous proposal on relativity in the scientific community, supported by hopelessly indoctrinated "priests of science," is seriously undercutting forward development in the fields of cosmology and physics (Hynecek 2009, 558).

Hynick's language is a not very subtle allusion to the clash between science and religion epitomized in the trial, condemnation, and suppression of Galileo and his work. The fact that it took almost 350 years for the Church to proclaim magisterially that the theologians were erroneous, and the scientists were correct, well illustrates the Galileo effect in religion. While a sainted Pope has definitively closed the book on the issue of heliocentrism and officially restored the good names of Copernicus and Galileo, an undercurrent of indifference and sometimes even distrust toward scientific learning endures among some Roman Catholic clergy and theologians. The Galileo effect in theology and ministry broadly persists. There is some irony here, given that the current pope holds a diploma in chemistry and has emphatically embraced the science that exposes the growing danger of global warming, especially in his encyclical on creation, *Laudato si'* (Italian, "Praise be to you [my Lord]"). More recently, science from fields of public health and immunology prompted dioceses to shutter the churches for public worship during the 2020 COVID-19 pandemic. If sciences can have such a public impact on even our ability to gather for worship, does not that bolster the case for allowing them to affect our pulpits as well?

One telling symbol of the dearth of scientific literacy among Roman Catholic ministers has been the work of various organizations to introduce the sciences into the theological curricula of today's seminaries and schools of ministry. One colleague directed a major grant focused on such an endeavor. The grant recognized that even though the conciliar document on priestly training from Vatican II affirmed the importance of the sciences when preparing ordination candidates (*Decree on Priestly Training*, 15), only about 8 percent of newly ordained priests have a strong background in the sciences. In an attempt to rectify that situation, one major grant funded the introduction of courses that linked theology and the sciences into college and pre-theology programs in selected Roman Catholic seminaries. At the end of the grant period, while affirming the great value of such courses, one participant asked a question distinctly pertinent to our consideration here: Can this material be preached?

> For priests to know something about advances in genetics, about an expanding universe, and about a congenial relationship between science and faith is not an option, but essential. People in the pew expect a clergy informed about the language of technology and science that dominates discourse these days.
>
> Doris Donnelly

Personally, I am no scientist and have precious little training in that area. High school chemistry was a nightmare, and college math was almost the undoing of my Capuchin vocation. While majoring in philosophy and the arts, I had to pass what I experienced as a grueling course in advanced math at our college seminary. During the final exam, the instructor walked by my desk, viewed my progress on the test with some consternation, and before walking away advised me that I should "stick to music!" While I eventually did graduate with a degree in music, I am nonetheless fascinated with the scientific world. I believe it to be a rich source for preaching, yet one largely untapped by the vast majority of Roman Catholic preachers today. Already in this text I have drawn upon at least a dozen scientific disciplines—from astronomy to entomology, from anthropology to neuroscience. I do so almost instinctively now because the many contributions from these and parallel disciplines have greatly enriched my ability to theologize, teach, and preach over the years. Maybe they can help your compound seeing as well.

Imagination and Nature's Sacramentality

Lutheran pastor David Lose is a masterful preacher and trustworthy homiletic guide. In his introduction to an essay on preaching and the imagination, he conjures an opening scene from George Bernard Shaw's play *Saint Joan*. In it, Joan has come to Robert de Baudricourt , a military leader, to solicit his support for her crusade against the English. During their conversation, Joan reveals that she hears voices directing her, and one such voice has specifically instructed her to seek Robert's help. He is somewhat taken aback by this disclosure and asks, "How do you mean? Voices?" "I hear voices telling me what to do," Joan replies, adding, "They come from God." Robert is unconvinced: "They come from your imagination." To which Joan answers, "Of course. That is how messages of God come to us." In commenting on that scene, Lose stresses that while many consider faith to be primarily about knowledge, it is also very much about imagination (Lose 2016, 190). Such is a crucial conduit for mediating the mystery of God's presence and framing a life consonant with that holy abiding.

In his exposition on preaching as "poetic seeing," the South African theologian Daniel Louw makes a similar point. He cites the often-invoked phrase of the twelfth-century Benedictine monk Anselm of Canterbury—*fides querens intellectum* or "faith seeking understanding." Over the centuries this phrase has established itself as the classic definition of theology itself. Louw recognizes that one dimension of preaching is enabling the Gospel message to be intelligible. While preaching is expected to be theological, it is also a strategic and distinctly practical form of theologizing that is meant to be more than a cognitive exercise. Our sermonizing is a proclamation of the very mission of God and a spiritual call to action. Louw characterizes this aspect of our preaching as *fides querens actum* or "faith seeking action." Spurring people into action, however, requires more than well-reasoned logic or compelling arguments. It also necessitates moving people's emotions, awakening their awe, and touching their hearts. For Louw, this is the process of *fides querens imaginem,* in which faith is fired through imagination (Louw, 1). Many scientists are aptly positioned to aid us in this endeavor by stimulating our imaginations about the created world, which Judeo-Christian revelation has affirmed as an unparalleled portal to the divine.

A preparatory step toward engaging the sciences as catalysts for our preaching might occur not only through pondering the created world but also by grasping something of its profound sacramentality. While Vatican II declared that the Church itself is a sacrament, and our tradition has taught since the Middle Ages that there are seven official sacraments of the Church, the concept of sacramentality is much broader and more ancient than that. In the early Church, sacramentality was a quite elastic framework. St. Augustine, for example, references more than three hundred actions and things as sacraments in his writings. This breadth is indicative of a Catholic spirituality that is foundationally a sacramental spirituality sustained by a sacramental imagination. A traditional expression of this Catholic mode of believing is found in the so-called *sacramental principle,* which holds that everything in the created world has the potential for revealing God. One of the more famous summations of this perspective was the instruction that St. Ignatius of Loyola, the founder of the Jesuits, gave to his followers: Go out and "find God in all things."

Pope Francis does not reference the created world in explicitly sacramental terms in his encyclical on care for our common home, *Laudato si'*. Nonetheless, his theologizing about the physical world leaves little doubt about his awareness of its foundational sacrality. For example, the pope teaches that "the entire material universe speaks of God's love. . . . Soil, water, mountains: everything is, as it were, is a caress of God" (84). He speaks of creation as a precious book that God has authored, and citing Pope St. John Paul II, teaches that the letters in that book "are the multitude of created things present in the universe." Drawing again on John Paul II, he stresses that alongside the revelation we find in Scripture, creation itself is a manifestation of the divine (85). Francis not only speaks of the sacredness of the world, but also asserts that beyond disclosing the presence of God, nature is in fact a locus of God's presence (88). It is not surprising, therefore, that toward the end of the encyclical the pope invites us to "discover God in all things" (233). Here his Jesuit spirituality converges with the Franciscan view that opens this encyclical; the title *Laudato si'* is a citation of the opening words of St. Francis of Assisi's famous *Canticle of Creation*. *Laudato si'* stands as a stunning reflection on the very sacramentality of the created world and a clarion call for us to respect and protect this wondrous gift.

Scientists and the Cosmic Sacrament

Margot Lee Shetterly's award-winning book, and later hit movie, *Hidden Figures*, brought to light the largely overlooked story of a group of African American women whose mathematical brilliance helped launch America into space, including Katherine Johnson, who used her considerable skills to calculate flight trajectories. Notably, she was able to solve essential equations for launching the capsule of John Glenn safely into orbit and returning it to earth, finding a solution that had evaded the engineers on the project—all White males. Johnson's solution was unusual, a form of math known as "Euler's Method," that allows scientists to imagine a solution to an equation that cannot be solved exactly. These calculated "approximations" did the trick.

One fallacy about the sciences—especially the so-called hard sciences such as math or chemistry—is that their methods are so data driven and their processes so rigorously empirical that there is little if any room left for speculation or mental artistry. Ironically, this view is sometimes espoused even by scientists themselves, who tend to downplay the imaginative and artistic aspects of their work. Often this is done to project an image of dispassionate research based only on the facts, which purportedly renders the findings more serious and thus more credible. Ironically, scientific legends such as Albert Einstein repeatedly noted the importance of imagination in scientific research. There are certain movements within various scientific communities today dedicated to reshaping the traditional dry-as-dust reporting of new discoveries into a more accessible and even exciting style of communication. One study goes so far as to emphasize how the teaching of science through storytelling renders it much more memorable and even transformative. Their research produced tangible evidence proving how imaginative and affective narratives are important to the understanding of science (Hadzigeorgiou, Klassen, and Klassen 2012, 1137).

> I am enough of an artist to draw freely upon my imagination. Imagination is more important than knowledge. Knowledge is limited. Imagination encircles the world.
>
> Albert Einstein

In a later chapter we will spend significant time on storytelling and its value in preaching. For now, it is worth noting that even scientists understand how dull reporting—or what could be classified as bad storytelling—diminishes the impact of sometimes earth-shattering discoveries. Preachers should pay attention to this reality, not only because it illumines an indispensable technique in the homiletic endeavor, but also because it opens our eyes to the possibility that various scientific discoveries can enhance our story telling and preaching.

For some, putting the words *science* and *interesting* in the same sentence seems contradictory. Consider, however, the physicist-cosmologist Stephen Hawking. His theorems and proofs were lauded by colleagues around the world, and he was awarded virtually every honor possible from the scientific community. He also wrote several works for the popular audience, including five volumes of children's fiction coauthored with his daughter, Lucy. His first popular work, *A Brief History of Time* (1988), spent a record breaking 273 weeks on the *Sunday Times'* bestseller list and to date has sold over 25 million copies in multiple languages. If such a monumental intellect could offer popular explanations about the mysteries of the universe, maybe learnings from him and his colleagues could help us introduce our assemblies to the mysteries of the very One who created the universe.

Nourishing this scientific way of seeing seems especially appropriate when preaching to adolescents and young adults. While I consider myself computer literate—I'm even certified as online teacher for higher education—digital is not my first language, as it is for so many young people today. How many of us rely on nieces or nephews, students, and other young folk to help us connect to the internet, get the HD television set up, or figure out the new cell phone. A number of years ago I gave my younger brother a Garmin GPS as he was about to launch into a road trip with his ten-year-old son. My brother was not quite sure how to operate the gadget, nor was I. When he asked for advice, I told him to give it to the ten-year-old, who had it figured out before they hit the highway. While young adults may be fleeing the Church in record numbers, they are not fleeing technology. Some sociologists and psychologists have even dubbed the generation born in the new millennium as the "iGeneration." The iGens (think iPhone) were born into media and technology usage like no other group. Not only are many of them fixated on electronic communication and media, they are also pursuing STEM studies—Science, Technology, Engineering, and Math— in ways unimaginable by preceding generations, even millennials. Learning science-speak, even if in halting and limited ways, might be an important bridge-building strategy in our preaching. It may also be one more way to heed Pope Francis' advice in moving away from staid patterns of thinking that may make sense only to us.

Zoology and Hearing God's Voice

Several years ago, a chance click of the television remote led me to a program documenting the work of Katy Payne, the founder of the "Elephant Listening Project," now housed at Cornell University in Ithaca, New York. Originally trained in both music and biology, she helped develop the field of bioacoustics, which studies the sounds animals use for communication. With her husband, Roger, she studied the singing of humpback whales. They came to understand that whales communicate through long, complex patterns that are similar to the songs of birds. Their work on whale songs brought them international recognition and remains an influential and highly regarded piece of research.

Later in her career, Payne was visiting the Portland Zoo when she felt, more than heard, a rumbling communication between two elephants standing on opposite sides of a concrete enclosure. She enlisted the help of two other acoustic biologists, who began to study and record these pachyderm conversations. Payne and her colleagues discovered that elephants vocally transmit at a very low frequency, dramatically below the threshold of human hearing. Her findings, popularized in the book *Silent Thunder*, document how these apparently silent giants have developed a sophisticated communication system, capable of broadcasting across many miles through African forests. Subsequently, the Elephant Listening Project was established at Cornell University. Their scientists and collaborators in the United States and in Africa continue the work now that Payne has retired. This work has emerged as a valuable tool for protecting elephants in their natural environments against poaching and environmental dangers.

Judeo-Christian revelation asserts that the God of Abraham and Sarah is the One who speaks and initiates dialogue, who constantly beckons us to love and conversion, and who calls us to eternal life. For Christians, the epitome of this divine vocalization is Jesus Christ, the one whom the Gospel of John proclaims as the enfleshed Word. On the other side of the equation, those same Scriptures recount how time and again humans have failed to hear, much less heed, the divine voice. They further enumerate the many ways we have ignored the sacred friendship echoing at the heart of this enduring annunciation. Our unfamiliarity with the Creator's voice is so extreme that some have the audacity to suggest that God no longer speaks, that the heavens are empty of any sacred presence, and by consequence, we no longer must listen for the divine call.

The work of a scientist like Katy Payne provides a useful set of spiritual metaphors for rethinking our individual and collective journey into the mystery of God. The empirical evidence demonstrates not that pachyderms are mute, but that our hearing is not calibrated to their frequency. They can hear each other, but we are sonically impaired in their

1 Samuel 3:3b–10, 19. How Eli helps Samuel hear God's voce.

The boy prophet is certainly eager to respond when called, but his inner ear is quite underdeveloped at this stage. He confuses God's call with a human summons. Ironically many of us do the opposite, often confusing human babble for holy discourse. As frequently, we are spiritually impaired, unable to detect echoes of the Spirit's summons in our lives.

Katy Payne is a gifted scientist, who with her husband, Roger, uncovered the songs of humpback whales. Years later, she deployed that same acoustic gift in a surprising discovery about elephant communication. While visiting a zoo in Portland, Oregon, she experienced a rumble between two elephants on either side of a concrete barrier. With the help of other acoustic biologists, she learned that elephants communicate at a frequency outside the range of human perception through infrasonic sound waves. In her book *Silent Thunder* she illustrates how these mammoth beasts can converse across long distances in the jungle, although their interactions are imperceptible to unsuspecting park rangers and other folk in the vicinity.

The prophet guardian Eli in today's first reading could be thought of as one who experienced some mystical calibration, allowing him to hear the silent thunder . . . the infrasonic invitation of the Holy One. This, in turn, allowed him to nudge the boy prophet into the very acoustic of God.

If your life is anything like mine, we have so much static in our lives . . . are so bombarded by the noise of criticism and greed . . . besieged by airwaves filled with so much self-promotion or self-protectionism, that God's voice gets lost in the static. It is muted by the acrimony of polarization, the undercurrent of racism, the demeaning of women. Thus, it is not only challenging to perceive what divine call might be coming our way, but sometimes even difficult to discern if God is speaking at all.

In the midst of this personal static and societal babble, we enter again the fellowship of disciples, submit to the holy thunder that echoes through today's Gospel, and confirm again that our God is never silent.

Homily excerpt, Second Sunday in Ordinary Time, Year B

environment. Analogously, our deafness to God's holy summons is not evidence of a silent divinity. Rather, it is symptomatic of our flawed ability to tune ourselves to the Holy Spirit and our limited aptitude for connecting to the salvific frequency revealed in Jesus. Many times our lectionary texts narrate some moment in salvation history when the divine invitation has elicited inadequate or even inert responses from us mortal creatures. In light of such texts, the work of scientists the likes of Katy Payne is a helpful tool for recalibrating our thinking about an apparently mute God. It reaffirms our foundational belief in the continued engagement of the Holy One in our world and in our lives. In turn, it offers a provocative avenue for addressing our ongoing work of personal and societal conversion with the eternal Word.

Auditory images are pervasive in Judeo-Christian revelation. While seeing becomes more important in the New Testament, hearing seems foundational for believing across the biblical literature. For example, the first word in the Jewish creed known as the Shema is *Hear!* (Deuteronomy 6:4). In a pivotal post-resurrection story, Jesus announces to Thomas the blessedness of those who cannot see but believe (John 20:29). Then there is Paul's stirring comments on discipleship in his Letter to the Romans:

> But how can they call on him in whom they have not believed? And how can they believe in him of whom they have not heard? And how can they hear without someone to preach? And how can people preach unless they are sent? As it is written, "How beautiful are the feet of those who bring [the] good news!" (Romans 10:14–15)

Maybe my musical training has sensitized me to the sonic quality of divine revelation, but I also believe this conviction is deeply rooted in the Scriptures. Sound is also the fundamental medium of our preaching. In an era that prizes visual pyrotechnics, exemplified by the massive screens that dominate sports venues and sometimes even our own homes, there are definite challenges for those of us engaged in a speaking-listening ministry. Helping people pay attention to sound as a cherished and particularly intimate medium of divine discourse is vital. The sciences can help us do that.

Paleontology, Neuroscience, and Pastoral Care

I first recognized a connection between the sciences and pastoral care when I accidentally stumbled across a story about a fossil from one of our human ancestors. Always in search of some fresh idea for my preaching or teaching, I was surprised to learn that paleontologists—those who study the ancient remains of a variety of living creatures from ferns to dinosaurs—concluded that distant relatives who lived a half a million years ago demonstrated the capacity for compassion. The reconstructed skull of a child, unearthed by a team of Spanish researchers, indicated that she or he would have been severely disabled at birth. Nonetheless, the child survived to at least five years old and possibly several years longer. The scientists concluded that the only way the youngster could have survived that long was that the family group cared for the child despite the obvious deformities. Some scientists contend that what they called "conspecific care," or what we might call compassion, is a unique trait of humans (Madrigal 2009). Other paleontologists have concurred. Notably studies of the fossil remains of *Homo erectus* demonstrate that this species not only cared for the young, but also for old, weak, and infirm individuals.

A gifted colleague of mine teaches across the fields of liturgy and pastoral care. One of his methods for the study of both is neuroscience, which is particularly concerned with the nervous system. His writings (Hogue 2017) introduced me to the work of psychologist Allan Schore, who researches brain development in infants. Schore describes the life of a newborn as somewhat chaotic, filled with unformed feelings and new sensations, and lacking any verbal comprehension of their world. According to Schore, the role of the nurturing parent is to mirror the infant's inner emotional life—the excitement, pain, joy, and sadness they experience—and give them both verbal and physical expression on the child's behalf. We have all done or at least observed that phenomenon, holding and soothing a child when she is crying or scared, patting their backs and making sympathetic sounds or singing soothing songs when they are upset. According to Schore, the nurturing parent helps strengthen and consolidate the child's awareness of her own feelings by amplifying them, usually through exaggeration. The parent is taking the chaotic and unformed feelings of the infant, ordering them, and then offering them back to the child. In a sense, using Schore's language, the parent is lending the child the use of her more mature brain as the child struggles to organize her experiences. In the process, the child's brain actually changes, as the neural bridge between the rational, problem-solving part of the brain and the emotional limbic system strengthens. Patterns of attachment and security through nurturing parents thus can be built into our brains and influence our ability to relate through the rest of our lives.

Many times the Gospel calls us to a level of discipleship that seems out of the reach of ordinary believers. It does not quite reduce us to infancy, but this divine invitation often looms beyond the capacity of our sometimes immature spiritualities. Living out discipleship is as difficult for us today as it was at the time of Jesus. Consequently, a pericope like that from the Gospel of Luke (12:32–48, "Blessed are those servants whom the master finds vigilant on his arrival") proclaimed on the Nineteenth Sunday in Ordinary Time in Year C might only increase our stress levels. It is tough enough to pay attention to the bills that come due, the relational demands of our families, and the unexpected challenges and even threats that living in today's world pose with such

> ## Gospel: Luke 12:32–48. Do not be afraid, yet be prepared like the prudent servant.
>
> The reason I make this excursion into neuroscience and parenting is to provide a way to think about a word that describes the flawless Son of God but at the same time is proclaimed to very flawed and imperfect disciples. Borrowing psychologist Schore's model, I would like to suggest that, like infants, we live in a somewhat chaotic world filled with violence and indignities, the brutalization of innocents, and a politics of derision that demeans all of us. Like a nurturing parent, the readings provide us a reassuring encounter with Jesus, who instead of offering us his prefrontal lobe to bring order to our chaotic emotional lives metaphorically lends us his divinely mature soul, his tempered faith, his shocking selflessness, and his comforting vision of God's reign to calm and steady us. Because of this nurturing Spirit, we can grow to be the faithful servants that our baptism summons us to be. We can live in grateful vigilance for the way God's own reign continues to break forth in our lives without fear.
>
> Homily excerpt, Nineteenth Sunday in Ordinary Time, Year C

regularity. On top of that, to stay alert to the demands of our own baptism and the apparent threat of divine judgment is formidable.

Schore's findings about the calming capacity of attentive parents and even their role in strengthening their children's brain structure are a powerful metaphor. While we are not infants, we are God's children, who lean on our brother Jesus for inspiration and leadership. We are a graced yet flawed people. Sometimes we and those we are privileged to serve are better at acknowledging our sin or inadequacy than admitting our own goodness or virtue. Fortuitously, our divine parent is always there to console and nurture us. What our Father lends us, however, is not part of the divine brain but, more importantly, the sacred heart of Jesus. Analogous to a parent's sharing of her emotional stability, God shares wisdom and moral stability in the example, teaching, and enduring presence of the Christ. The more we embrace this steadying gift, the more we are spiritually strengthened and consoled. Considering the revelation of Luke 12, we remain vigilant not because God is going to ambush us with judgment, but because the Holy One lavishes us with an abiding and loving Spirit. In the process, we mature in our capacity to live out that steadying and strengthening gift in our own lives and in turn extend it to others.

Chaos Theory and Ethics

The 1993 blockbuster film *Jurassic Park,* based on Michael Crichton's 1990 novel, introduced the concept of chaos theory to the masses. In this tale, the leading advocate of the theory was the self-styled "chaotician" Ian Malcolm, played by Jeff Goldblum. Early in the film, Malcolm disputes the approach that the billionaire John Hammond, played by Richard Attenborough, and his scientists had taken to cloning dinosaurs and displaying them in a theme park. Hammond insisted that it was possible to control the newly resurrected species; the scientists had genetically engineered all the dinosaurs to be females so they could not reproduce on their own. Malcolm refutes Hammond's claim to be able to harness the power of evolution. His ominous, prophetic words haunt the rest of the film: "Life finds a way."

Much of the work behind chaos theory is embedded in the dense calculations of mathematicians who were attempting to predict planetary movements at the dawn of the twentieth century. In related work, other theoretical mathematicians were studying unexpected complications in simple formulas. Some scientists theorized that they could use such formulas to predict, for example, how objects would act in gravity. The development of advanced computers in the mid-twentieth century provided the means to forever challenge such theories.

The work of meteorologist Edward Lorenz, who is sometimes called the father of chaos theory, was pivotal in this development. Lorenz sought to understand the chaotic behavior in weather and tried, with little success, to create a mathematical model that could accurately predict the weather. While running an experiment on weather modeling in 1961 at the Massachusetts Institute of Technology, Lorenz discovered that the variation of even one thousandth (.001) of a decimal number in his calculations would render vastly different results. He concluded, to his own surprise, "any physical system that behaved nonperiodically would be unpredictable" (Gleick 1987, 18). His insight is sometimes referred to as the "butterfly effect." Lorenz himself used that phrase in a lecture he offered at the 1972 conference of the American Association

---

Luke 10:25–37. Who is my neighbor?

While Jesus is not exactly a chaotician, his parables did create unexpected pandemonium among his hearers about the nature of God and who was destined for divine favor. Some religious leaders of his time thought they could determine the nature of holiness and so shaped very clear rules about cleanliness and purity that could restrict those they considered unworthy from accessing Divine Presence and the community of the Chosen.

Chaos theory, made famous in the movie Jurassic Park, reminds us of the unpredictability of our universe. You have probably heard the shorthand for this theory as the "butterfly effect": A butterfly flaps its wings in Brazil and we get tornados in the Midwest. Closer to home, think about the last snowstorm and the trillions of snowflakes that blanketed the city. In the turbulence of wind currents, as ice crystals randomly adhere to each other and fall to the ground, we are covered in a blizzard of unimaginable diversity, as no two snowflakes are alike.

continued next page...

Jesus envisions a similar chaos in the turbulent task of discerning who our neighbor is. We instinctively gravitate towards those who look like us, or think like us, or vote like us. The Jesus world is more tumultuous, in which no two human beings are identical, but each uniquely reflects the Divine Image. In this blizzard of humanity we are blanketed in the unimaginable diversity of humankind, the crown of all creation.

Poet and preacher Barbara Brown Taylor pushes hard when commenting on this text. She disallows Christians to use it as a self-congratulatory tale for thinking we have the right answer about being neighborly. She asserts our blindness in missing the fact that the Samaritan was the enemy, not one of us; he belonged to the other side. In underscoring the revolting nature of this heroic Samaritan to Jewish sensibilities, Taylor asks, "Who is the last person in the world you would want to give you CPR? the kind of person you would hate to thank for saving your life?" That's our own Good Samaritan. And, as Taylor reminds us, when we are lying in a ditch after being beaten and robbed, anyone who stops to help is our new best friend.

Jesus the chaotician discombobulates our neat categories of friend and foe, neighbor and enemy, saint and sinner. In this holy pandemonium the Jesus invitation is live in sacred openness to the expected neighbor poised to pull us from that metaphorical ditch that we might live more abundantly.

Homily excerpt, Fifteenth Sunday in Ordinary Time, Year C

for the Advancement of Science, titled "Predictability: Does the Flap of a Butterfly's Wings in Brazil Set Off a Tornado in Texas?"

In chapter 2, St. Augustine's revealing insight about the challenge of trying to explain God was discussed: *Si comprehendis, non est Deus* (roughly translated, "If you think you understand it, it's not God!" Sermon 117). Chaos theory helps us recognize without needing to explain the baffling mystery of God. Theologian James Huchingson summons the image of the formless abyss described in Genesis 1:2 — which he calls *"pandemonium tremendum"* — to speak about the holy pandemonium through which we perceive God (Huchingson 2001, xx). Jesus certainly introduced a holy pandemonium into the Judaism of his day, particularly by embracing the unclean and by welcoming public sinners into his inner circle The parable of the Good Samaritan offers a proto-type of this disruptive reconfiguring of community and the Godhead. Scripture scholar John Dominic Crossan suggested that it took Jesus at least an hour to tell this parable, which takes only eight verses in the Gospel of Luke (Luke 10:30–37). That imagined elongation might have occurred not because we have lost segments of the text but because of all the arguments that might have broken out as Jesus unfolded the story. Members of the priestly Levites would have seriously objected to his characterizations of their representatives in the tale. When Jesus revealed the Samaritan as the bearer of mercy and love, the whole crowd must have erupted in a holy uproar (Crossan 2012, 90).

Preaching that parable raises equally problematic questions today about who our neighbor might be. In an era of increasing polarization and eroding civility, it is tough to imagine one of "them"—some polit-ical or religious or ethnic other—to be our neighbor. In such a discon-certing environment, chaos theory provides a useful metaphor for the topsy-turvy community Jesus envisions for his followers. In his world, we do not get to choose our neighbors, just as that Jewish traveler knocked into the ditch on the road from Jerusalem to Jericho did not. Instead, God chooses every human being as the new Samaritan and the unexpected messenger of sacred kindness, no matter how shockingly different they may be from the one they have been chosen for. When Christians embrace this holy bedlam, we promise the world a different butterfly effect, one in which random love and unexpected care announce the in-breaking of God's reign. Malcolm was right: Life will break through. For Christians, that means that Christ can break through in the unpredictability of our own living and loving.

The Psychology of Gratitude

Parents and grandparents frequently coax manners and broader social awareness into little ones by reminding them to say thank you. How many times did I hear my parents, and now my siblings, say to children and grandchildren, "And what do you say?" after the bestowal of some gift, large or small. While such coaching is aimed at developing social graces in a child, it also might be contributing to their mental health and personal well-being. There is reliable scientific evidence about the value of an appreciative spirit. Dr. Robert Emmons, a professor of psychology at the University of California Davis, is a leading expert on this science of gratitude. In a series of studies, Emmons and his colleagues have demonstrated that cultivating thankfulness is not only a useful social strategy, but it also produces physical as well as psychological benefits (Emmon 2007).

One experiment that Emmons and his colleagues conducted over a thousand times with people from eight to eighty years old utilized what he calls "gratitude journals." This procedure invited people to record on a regular basis the things for which they are grateful. It is a practice I first learned from a wonderful mentor who was confronted with an aggressive cancer that overturned and eventually took her life. Every day throughout her chemo and radiation treatments, at the suggestion of her oncologist, Connie would write down five new things for which she was grateful. It was challenging to keep brainstorming fresh triggers for her gratitude, especially after she abandoned extraordinary medical interventions and moved into hospice. She had to dig deep. One example that I cherish is her reflection on sleepless nights in a warm and increasingly uncomfortable bed, then turning the pillow over and experiencing the refreshing coolness of its other side. In the end, her daily list was filled only with people's names as she searched every corner of her memory to recover the faces of the many individuals who had been a grace in her life.

Emmons contends that there is empirical proof of the value of this practice. Connie often commented how it enabled her to envision her life as a very privileged and joyful one, even as it slipped away. Cultivating an appreciative attitude also produces positive physiological effects such as generating higher levels of positive emotions, increasing our alertness, and rendering us more optimistic. These are immense gifts for someone battling surgeries, chemotherapy, and radiation. Scientists also contend that increasing our gratitude strengthens our immune systems, lowers our blood pressure, and contributes to sounder and more refreshing sleep. Other studies have demonstrated that there are economic and environmental boons to this practice, such as reports that businesses that are intentional about communicating their gratitude to their clientele generate a more loyal customer base (Hasan 2014). Some social science

Luke 17:11–19. "Where are the other nine? Was there no one to return and give thanks to God except this foreigner?"

I have joked with my siblings that this was our mother's favorite Gospel. She was not only "old school"; I think she was one of its founders. "Please" and "thank you" were deeply embedded in our DNA. Looking back, however, the primary motivation for this "Foley-speak" was not guilt but love. Many years later, as we handed over our parents to God, it was abundant gratitude in that love that mitigated virtually every grief.

Social scientists like Dr. Robert Emmons confirm that gratitude does more than mollify parents or socially placate others in authority. Rather, an appreciative attitude contributes to better mental and physical health. Enumerating even the smallest reasons for thankfulness each day can help lower our blood pressure and boost our optimism. I learned the practice from a dear friend battling cancer. It became a life-giving exercise, as she daily envisioned five things, events, and eventually only people as affirming presences for which she joyfully gave thanks.

For Jesus, gratitude was more than a psychologically useful practice. Instead, the Only-Begotten embraced it at the core of his spirituality. His gratitude was manifest in embracing creation and creatures as distinctive revelations of the Father's enduring love. Every time he gathered disciples to a meal—whether an intimate event or el fresco dining with thousands—he gave thanks over bread and wine. He demonstrated that gratitude is a form of paying attention to God's loving spirit in our midst that missions us to help others recognize the same. In today's Gospel, practicing gratitude is particularly highlighted on the borders not only of Samaria and Galilee, but on the borders between health and illness, love and conflict, holiness and sinfulness, and even life and death, where it does not elicit guilt but offers holy comfort.

Homily excerpt, Twenty-Eighth Sunday in Ordinary Time, Year C

studies indicate that there is even an empirical relationship between gratitude and materialism: enhanced gratitude renders human beings less materialistic. A collateral benefit here is that a decrease in materialism in a significant number of people drains our natural resources at a slower rate and is kinder to the environment (Lambert 2009).

One famous story of apparent ingratitude in the Scriptures is Luke's narrative of Jesus meeting ten lepers on the border between Samaria and Galilee (Luke 17:11–19). While all are healed, only the Samaritan returns. Jesus wonders aloud about the missing nine and underscores the irony that the only messenger of thankfulness was an outsider and celebrated enemy of the Jews. A surface reading of this text could prompt preachers to use it as holy ammunition for prodding the baptized into being more grateful. I heard one unnamed homilist cajole, "Consequently, we must be grateful to God and the Church and the clergy because of all the things we do for you." The rising guilt at that moment in that assembly was almost palpable; it certainly increased my shame factor. A more thoughtful approach, such as contextualizing that pericope in the deep prayer traditions of Christianity, points to a more gracious revelation.

At the very heart of Christian worship is Eucharist, which in the original Greek is a verb that literally means "to give thanks." We are reminded of this foundational definition at the outset of each Eucharistic Prayer, when the preface dialogue urges, "Let us give thanks to the Lord our God," with the people affirming that to do so is both "right and just." Gratitude is not simply a religious courtesy or a groveling response in the face of eternal graciousness. Holding to that motivation for thanks reduces the baptized to menial creatures forever trapped by our eternal indebtedness to God. Conversely, one of the earliest Eucharistic texts in the west—ascribed to Hippolytus of Rome (d. 235) and the basis of our Eucharistic Prayer II—counters with texts that proclaim the baptized as recipients of God's own Spirit and worthy to stand in his presence and serve him. Although we are undeserving, Jesus has called us friends (John 15:15). Gratitude in view of this gift is less about groveling and more about awe.

This call to thankfulness, central to every Mass, summons us to a distinctive spirituality disposing us to perceive God's radiating presence "in good times and bad," as the Marriage rite puts it. Cultivating gratitude for the sake of human flourishing also builds our capacity to pay attention to God's enduring graciousness, even and especially when we are disinclined to acknowledge it. Gratitude so calibrated not only lowers our human anxieties, it also boosts our spiritual optimism about a God whose graciousness could never abandon us.

Conclusion

South African President Nelson Mandela decided to learn the language of his oppressors during his twenty-seven years in prison. While his native tongue was Xhosa and he was fluent in English, he dedicated himself to learning Afrikaans. This became a source of tension between himself and some of fellow prisoners. He explained that he did this to negotiate more effectively with prison officials about the harsh conditions of his and his compatriot's confinement. More importantly, he explained, he did it so that he could read the literature and poetry of his oppressors and come to understand more intimately the minds of those who built and maintained the apartheid system.

Most Roman Catholic clergy today do not speak science even as a second or third language. Most of us received a liberal arts education, and often our major was philosophy. Every study of higher education today indicates that degrees in the liberal arts are vanishing at an astonishing pace. In the period after Vatican II, when clergy education was under serious renewal, 20 percent of all degrees in the United States were granted in the humanities. Virtually all priesthood candidates received their undergraduate training in philosophy, as many still do. Today less than 5 percent of college student major in the humanities. While between 2006 and 2016 there was an almost 38-percent increase in the number of baccalaureate degrees awarded, the number of students in majors such as education, English, philosophy, and languages dropped dramatically. Not surprising, the STEM disciplines—science, technology, engineering, and math—experienced the greatest increase in graduates (Nietzel 2019). This is the generation that the Church is losing in droves and who, Pope Francis reminds us, must be heard in new and intentional ways. Learning to "speak science," even if halting or inadequately, is an important channel for communicating to contemporary assemblies.

In this vein, scientists could be appreciated as a new kind of Good Samaritan for preachers. It is true that some in the pulpit, as well some as in politics, believe that scientists are at least the "other," if not the enemy. Chalk it up to the enduring Galileo effect. For me, however, they are resources who can help me out of the preaching rut that I sometimes dig myself into. Those of us who engage in this ministry with some regularity can easily run out of ideas. Unfortunately, that does not stop us from preaching. Thus, we sometimes wear out our hearers with the same ideas, the same stories, and the same language we have been deploying for years or even decades. Replenishing the imagination is essential for preachers and for our assemblies.

Towards the end of his life, the celebrated chemist Friedrich August Kekulé (d. 1896) delivered a lecture to a group of aspiring young scientists. In that presentation he urged them to "note every footprint, every bent twig, every fallen leaf, and there you will see where next to place your feet." He called this way of doing science—and science itself—as a form of pathfinding (Ingold 2018). We might also imagine our homilizing as a kind of pathfinding in which we accompany our assemblies as they journey into the mystery of God in Christ. Maybe along the way we might lean on those scientific minds and imaginative spirits who help us look more closely at the twigs and leaves, the atoms and quarks, the planets and the galaxies. In the process, the pathway to holiness might be newly illuminated and surprisingly revealed.

References

Crossan, John Dominic. 2012. *The Power of Parable: How Fiction by Jesus Became Fiction about Jesus,* New York: HarperCollins.

Emmon, Robert A. 2007. *Thanks! How Practicing Gratitude Can Make You Happier.* New York: Houghton Mifflin Harcourt.

Francis, Pope. 2015. Encylical letter, *Laudato si': On Care for Our Common Home.* http://www.vatican.va/content/francesco/en/encyclicals/documents/papa-francesco_20150524_enciclica.

Gleick, James. 1987. *Chaos: Making a New Science.* New York: Viking Penguin.

Hadzigeorgiou, Yannis, Stephen Klassen, and Catherine Froese Klassen. 2012. "Encouraging a 'Romantic Understanding' of Science: The Effect of the Nikola Tesla Story." *Science and Education* 21, no. 8: 1111–1138.

Hasan, Fazal E. Syed, Ian Lings, Larry Neale, and Gary Mortimer. 2014. "The Role of Customer Gratitude in Making Relationships Marketing Investments Successful." *Journal of Retailing and Consumer Services* 21, no. 5: 788–796.

Hebron, John. 2010. *Galileo.* Oxford: Oxford University Press.

Hogue, David. 2017. "Because We Are: Practical Theology, Intersubjectivity and the Human Brain." *Practicing Ubuntu: Practical Theological Perspectives on Injustice, Personhood and Human Dignity.* Ed. Jaco Dreyer et al., 181–191. Berlin: LIT Verlag.

Huchingson, James. 2001. *Pandemonium tremendum: Chaos and Mystery in the Life of God*. Cleveland: Pilgrim Press.

Hynecek, Jaroslav. 2009. "The Galileo Effect and the General Relativity Theory." *Physics Essays* 22, no. 4: 551–559.

Ingold, Tim. 2017. "The Art of Paying Attention." Keynote lecture at The Art of Research Conference, Helsinki. https://www.youtube.com/watch?v=2Mytf4ZSqQs.

John Templeton Foundation. "Integrating Science into College and Pre-Theology Programs in US Roman Catholic Seminaries." https://www.templeton.org/grant/integrating-science-into-college-and-pre-theology-programs-in-us-rc-seminaries-2.

Lambert, Nathaniel, Frank Fincham, Tyler Stillman, and Lukas Dean. 2009. "More Gratitude, Less Materialism: The Mediating Role of Life Satisfaction" *The Journal of Positive Psychology* 2, no. 1: 32–42.

Louw, Daniel. 2016. "Preaching as art (imaging the unseen) and art as homiletics (verbalizing the unseen)." *HTS Teologiese Studies/Theological Studies* 72, no. 2. http://dx.doi.org/10.4102/hts.v72i2.3826.

Lose, David. 2016. "Imagination and Preaching." In *A Handbook for Catholic Preaching*. Ed. Edward Foley, 190–199. Collegeville, MN: Liturgical Press.

Madrigal, Alexis. 2009. "Deformed Skull Suggests Human Ancestors Had Compassion." *Wired* (March 30, 2009). https://www.wired.com/2009/03/skull/.

Nietzel, Michael. 2019. "Whither the Humanities: The Ten-Year Trend in College Majors." *Forbes* (January 7, 2019). https://www.forbes.com/sites/michaeltnietzel/2019/01/07/whither-the-humanities-the-ten-year-trend-in-college-majors/#4a58556964ad.

Payne, Katy. 1998. *Silent Thunder*. New York: Simon and Schuster.

Schore, Allan. 1994. *Affect Regulation and the Origin of the Self: The Neurobiology of Emotional Development*. Hillsdale, NJ: Lawrence Erlbaum Associates.

Taylor, Barbara Brown. 2013. "Sermon: The Right Answer." Riverside Church, New York. https://www.youtube.com/watch?v=wds3OxzHNAI.

Thoreau, Henry David. 2013. *The Essential Thoreau*. New York: Simon and Schuster.

CHAPTER
5

The Arts in the Pulpit

It is simply natural that plain attention is a piety and that
the unaggressive articulation of attention in poems may be a form
of prayer, an instance of worship.

~Donald Revell

D amon Tweedy received his medical degree from Duke University,
where he also completed his residency in psychiatry. He also holds
a law degree from Yale University. His memoir, *Black Man in a White
Coat: A Doctor's Reflections on Race and Medicine,* takes the reader on
an eye-opening trek through the medical world and its often-hidden
prejudices. Tweedy did not get his undergraduate degree from some
fancy Ivy League institution but found his way into Duke's Medical
School through an affirmative action program. One of the few students
of color in his cohort in the 1990s, Tweedy's self-effacing work illumi-
nates rampant racism in our medical system through personal stories
narrated with a quiet yet fierce honesty. He even admits his own prejudices when treating African Americans patients. A persistent drumbeat
throughout the book is that being black can be bad for your health.

While endlessly fascinating, the book was a difficult read for me.
One memorable story from Tweedy's first year of medical school hit me
hard. It occurred halfway through his first semester. Though Tweedy
did not have the economic or educational advantages of most of his
classmates, he was in the top half of his class on each of his midterm
exams. He started to believe that he actually belonged at Duke. Then,
during, a break in one of his classes, the professor descended from the

stage and headed in his direction. Ordinarily this professor did not socialize with students, but he nonetheless made a beeline for Tweedy.

"Are you here to fix the lights?" he asked.

The sounds of the classroom seemed to vanish. So did my peripheral vision. Calm down, I told myself, maybe he was talking to someone else and only seemed to be looking at me. . . . Maybe with all the background noise, I had misheard him.

"Did . . . did you ask me about fixing the lights?" I said.

"Yes," he replied, irritation creeping into his voice. "You can see how dim it is over on that side of the room," he said, gesturing with his index finger. "I called about this last week."

Reflexively, I stroked my chin and looked down at my clothing to check if I seemed out of place. Clean-shaven, and dressed in polo shirt and khaki slacks, I thought that I'd done a decent job of looking the part of the preppy first-year medical student. Obviously I had failed.

"No," I said, stumbling to come up with a reply. "I don't have anything to do with that."

He frowned. "Then what are you doing here in my class?"

My mouth went dry. Why had he intentionally singled me out in this way? Race was the first thought that entered my mind. I tried to summon an attitude of 1960s-era Black Power defiance, but what came out sounded like 1990s diffidence. "I'm a student . . . in your class."

"Oh . . . " he said. Dr. Gale looked away, then walked off without another word. I staggered to my seat, sitting through the second part of his lecture like a robot, tuning out his voice. What had started out as a promising day was spoiled. (Tweedy 2015, 12–13)

Some commentators have imaginatively reframed storytelling as a kind of mental or emotional simulator. It is common practice today for airline pilots, student drivers, and even surgical interns to hone their skills on a whole range of computerized contrivances that allow them to operate with little risk to themselves or anyone else. In a parallel fashion, as we listen to a story, we immerse ourselves in the narration and vicariously experience the insights and emotions of its characters without imperiling ourselves. While some contend that making our way through another's memoir, a work of science fiction, or even well-crafted history is a suspension of reality, it is actually an expansion of it.

I was not in the room when Damon Tweedy's dignity was abused by his unreflective instructor. Nonetheless, when reading this incident I felt shock, empathy, and eventually rage. *Black Man in a White Coat* allowed me an imperfect yet authentic glimpse of the devastating effects of systemic racism. As with many other art forms, great writing lures us into an unforeseen world where our senses are heightened, our emotions are aroused, and sometimes our hearts are ripped opened.

While it is not our ordinary frame of reference, the Liturgy of the Word can similarly be treated as a form of spiritual simulation. As Matthew's Gospel unfolds, for example, we not only witness Peter's seaside call to follow Jesus (Matthew 4:18–19), we also feel the affirmation in that call and later the stinging reversal as Jesus rebukes his chosen "rock" (16:18) as "Satan" (16:23). We not only listen to the parable of a prodigal father and inheritance-snatching sons but instinctively insert ourselves in this powerful tale—frequently aligning ourselves with the slighted older brother (Luke 15:25–32). Preaching also invites a kind of simulated future in which the baptized reimagine themselves as a more perfect community of the beloved (Mark 1:11), ponder living the beatitudes with fresh zeal (Matthew 5:1–11), and even defy death itself by standing with the crucified in public witness (John 19:25–27).

After the death of the poet Robert Frost in 1963, President John F. Kennedy delivered a speech at Amherst College in the poet's honor just months before his own assassination. In that tribute, Kennedy hymned the potency of the arts in general and poetry in particular for shaping a more virtuous and moral society.

When power leads man toward arrogance, poetry reminds him of his limitations. When power narrows the areas of man's concern, poetry reminds him of the richness and diversity of his existence. When power corrupts, poetry cleanses, for art establishes the basic human truths which must serve as the touchstones of our judgment. . . . I see little of more importance to the future of our country and our civilization than full recognition of the place of the artist. If art is to nourish the roots of our culture, society must set the artist free to follow his vision wherever it takes him.

John F. Kennedy, 1964

Civic leaders, educators, and philanthropists have long grasped the power of the arts for nurturing the human spirit and orientating a society to larger truths. Over the centuries, the Church, as a consistent patron of the arts, has also admitted and promoted their influence. However, not every artistic deployment is an exercise of virtue, and the motivations for patronage by church and society are not always pure. It is well recognized, for example, that Adolph Hitler and his Third Reich effectively recruited a wide range of artists for his propaganda machine. Promoting idealized images from ancient Greek and Roman cultures served their perverse vision of Aryan superiority. It also served to justify artistically the extermination of Jews, the disabled, and anyone else who did not measure up to these paradigms.

The selection of art can also be an act of elitism and a form of social snobbery. For example, the endless debates about which music is worthy of inclusion in Roman Catholic liturgy pivot on definitions of beauty and the often unacknowledged power issues underlying such disputes. Who is actually empowered to regulate artistic standards for the people at worship? "Beauty according to whom?" is an enduring liturgical and cultural question in these discussions. Even Andrew Greeley's useful work on the link between the Catholic imagination and the fine arts, explored in chapter 3, carries some of these elitist overtones. Notice that his correlation was between Roman Catholics and the so-called fine arts. Conversely, what is the connection between catholicity, which in the broadest sense means universal, and those more common artistic expressions that the masses find so entertaining? Nathan Mitchell brings his incisive wit to bear on the complex matter of standards and aesthetics when he quips, "Secretly, many of us believe that God loves the poor, but hates their art. Surely, we suspect, God prefers Mozart to Randy Travis" (Mitchell 1996, 258).

Like preaching itself, every artistic evaluation is a contextual exercise. Those of us who engage in the homiletic enterprise are by definition called to a form of theologizing that respects the tastes and cultural expressions of our parochial assemblies. At the same time, the myriad of artistic forms ranging from folk art to fine arts may supply surprising tools for expanding the faithful's spiritual imaginations. These media allow virtual simulations both for thinking about religious ideas and for acting out our faith in a relatively safe environment. This is a great boon in the admittedly risky business of living the Christian life.

Human Dignity Meets *Frozen*

A trek into the arts at the service of preaching could begin with a consideration of a revered Renaissance painting such as Raphael's *School of Athens,* created for the Vatican's Apostolic Palace between 1509 and 1511. An equally sophisticated launch into the topic might find us pondering one of the uplifting oratorios of the classical composer Franz Joseph Haydn (d. 1809), such as his *Creation,* or the more frequently performed and widely loved *Messiah* by G. F. Handel (d. 1759). While I have employed the works of these virtuosos in my preaching and teaching, my starting point here is a more unlikely one: film. I do so for two reasons. First is the global popularity of this medium. The worldwide saturation of this art form was demonstrated by the fact that films from ninety-three countries were submitted for consideration for the Best International Feature Film category for a recent Academy Award. Besides the usual submissions from such places as Italy and India, entries came from Haiti, Malta, Laos, Uzbekistan, and some countries that I did not even know existed, such as the Kingdom of Bhutan. More remarkably, the Academy of Motion Picture Arts and Sciences awarded the Oscar for best picture to a non-English film, the Korean production *Parasite.* The movie industry is not just a global phenomenon; it also generates staggering profits. Recently the income generated by movie studios in the United States alone produced more wealth than the gross domestic product of over half of the countries in the world.

Paying attention to film is fruitful for preachers because of its capacity for drawing moviegoers into the narrative and deeply engrossing them in a story. While opera and dance have traditionally been considered the most multimedia artistic forms, movies are undoubtedly the most immersive artistic simulators available to the general public. While not quite as enveloping as a virtual reality system, it is for most people the closest option for such immersion. Admittedly, not every moviegoer is equally enraptured with every feature. You may have been bored with each succeeding segment of the *Star Wars* saga or with whatever other release that Hollywood touted as its latest blockbuster. Nonetheless,

they are natural storytellers and budding theologians. The plot revolves around two sisters, Elsa and Anna, and Elsa's stunning power to create ice and snow. The subsequent freezing of a kingdom, interwoven with acts of greed and power mongering, ultimately culminates in a tale about the power of love to melt the physical and metaphorical ice of land and hearts.

During an unusually contentious moment in public discourse, I found that movie and its characters a penetrating counterpoint for considering our baptismal vocation to be salt and light. While we were not in a meteorological deep freeze—as sometimes happens in Chicago—we were nonetheless in a kind of polar vortex that seemed to be stalled over our political leaders, our society, our basic civility. It was almost as though you could hear Elsa blasting the lyrics of "Let It Go" in the background: a text that embraces an instinct for slamming doors, demonstrates studied indifference to raging storms, and is at least apathetic if not cruel in its embrace of subzero temperatures and their lethal potential for ravaging the human body and spirit.

Yet, as I attempted to communicate in the homily, we did not enter the baptismal font to learn such a song. As citizens of this world and the next (*Constitution on the Church in the Modern World*, 43) such social and political ice storms should bother us.

What was useful for me from this Disney fantasy were the well-recognized set of metaphors and symbols from the tale that could be translated into Gospel challenges. In the preaching I did not attempt to affirm the quality or morality of the movie or promote it further. Rather, I hoped to capitalize on images and music well embedded in the minds of kids, their parents, and even grandparents as an unexpected springboard for nurturing the mission of the baptized to be light and salt in our challenging world. Disney's imagineers may have only intended to create entertainment for the masses, but for me they provided a potent fantasy world that I could deploy in the service of our own Masses and the holy mysteries they weekly celebrate.

Black Elk and Fools for Christ

Because academic life requires so much reading, I need other ways of feeding my imagination that are both refreshing and inexpensive. One reliable substitute has been listening to audio books. Many of these can be downloaded without cost from a local library or accessed through various subscription services. The service that I mainly rely upon allows me to return any book that I find disappointing and receive a full refund without any penalty. That feature frees me to be more adventuresome and opt for selections that I might otherwise avoid. While this gamble has not always paid off, most of the time I am both delighted and stretched by these unexpected finds.

The plight of Native Americans in our country is something I have learned about from colleagues and members of my religious community who have served them over the years. For decades, one of my Capuchin brothers has ministered to the Crow people in Montana and has even become a recognized expert in their language. He was one of the inspirations behind my decision to listen to Joe Jackson's new biography, *Black Elk: The Life of an American Visionary*. The other was recent news that the Catholic bishops of the United States had given their approval for opening a formal cause for the canonization of this Lakota medicine man turned Catholic catechist. Digging into his history and that of his people seemed a timely thing to do.

This sprawling biography does more than introduce us to this one-time Sioux warrior and close relative to the war leader Crazy Horse. Black Elk was an eyewitness to the Battle of Little Bighorn in 1876; participated in Buffalo Bill's Wild West show in England, where he met Queen Victoria in the late 1880s; and fought at the Wounded Knee Massacre in 1890. His life story serves as a vivid introduction to important slices of Native American history. This includes the checkered history of Christians trying to convert indigenous individuals and tribes, as well as our government's dishonest and demeaning treatment of these original Americans.

Black Elk is an unusual figure for a variety of reasons. What I found especially intriguing was the way his life bridged Native American and Christian religious practices and beliefs. An honored medicine man among his people, he experienced mystical visions at an early age that were harbingers of the holiness and wisdom that would develop throughout his life. He practiced traditional healing arts and participated in indigenous rituals, including the banned Sun Dance. In his early forties

Black Elk was baptized, taking the name Nicholas. He eventually became a catechist and lay missionary. While some contend that he abandoned all traditional forms of medicine when he was baptized, Jackson tells the tale in such a way that these two streams seem to converge within him and complement each other.

Black Elk had learned through a vision when he was nineteen years old that he was destined to be a *Heyoka*. Among the Lakota people, this is the most celebrated and difficult of all sacred roles. A *Heyoka* is a kind of sacred clown and contrarian. As a holy fool, he is free to ask difficult questions and to say what others are afraid to say. *Heyoka* are mirrors and teachers who employ extreme behaviors like wearing clothes inside out or riding backwards on their horses. In these gestures of lunatic wisdom, they shock people into reflecting upon the craziness of their own lives and decisions. In the mirror of the *Heyoka,* others are enticed into imagining a foolish future beyond their own doubts and fears, their collective inadequacies, and personal weaknesses.

While it might seem counterintuitive, I find the major feasts of the Church year the most difficult to preach. Their themes are so familiar and their scriptural readings so repetitive, that I am hard pressed to find some fresh take on preaching for the likes of Christmas and Pentecost. Occasionally I will hold onto a story or metaphor for months in anticipation of these festivals. It was during Lent that I listened to the audiobook of Jackson's *Black Elk*. His exploration of Black Elk's ministry as a *Heyoka* and the necessary sacrifices of this most challenging medicine practice immediately grabbed my attention. St. Paul's reference to himself as a fool for Christ came to mind. With Triduum and Easter looming on the horizon, however, it occurred to me that long before St. Paul, Jesus was our original *Heyoka*. By a happy coincidence, Easter fell on April Fool's Day that year. More than providing the opportunity for a clever metaphor, however, it fed my concern about preaching Resurrection as more than a great relief after the challenges of Lent and Good Friday. Baptism is an invitation to begin living the paschal mystery in service to others, as did Jesus. That may make us look foolish in the eyes of the world, but such is necessary for Christians who wager on resurrection. For those of us who preach, this is an invitation

St. Paul has a befuddling line in his First Letter to the Corinthians, where he calls himself a fool for Christ. It is not a phrase that has previously resonated with me. When listening to Joe Jackson's biography of Black Elk, however, it dawned on me that Paul wasn't the original fool: Jesus was. This only-begotten *Heyoka* was a contrarian to stilted traditional practices and beliefs: touching the unclean, consorting with Samaritan women, and disclosing a God enamored with sinners. So they killed him for his public foolishness. Being God's fool was the risk he took in life and the one he offers us in the promise of resurrection.

Resurrection does not vindicate the status quo or justify going along with the crowd. Rather, like Jesus, it calls us to gamble on the other, the marginalized, the outcast. And so there's the Easter oops, the resurrectional rub, the challenge of this central feast that falls on April Fool's Day for the first time in sixty years. Today we are invited not simply into what a young relative calls Easter-fool's day, but the invitation to an Easter-fool's life in which we continue to proclaim good news to the poor, freedom for prisoners, and set the oppressed free so that resurrection is more than a future hope but begins as a present reality.

Homily excerpt, Easter 2018

to become a kind of wise fool who dares to embrace preaching as a ministry of holy foolishness.

Music and the Dance of God

Herman Wouk was a Pulitzer Prize winning novelist, best known for works of historical fiction such as *The Caine Mutiny*. In his research for a second novel on World War II, Wouk interviewed a series of scientists involved in developing the atomic bomb. One of them was the theoretical physicist Richard Feynman, a prominent figure in the organization that oversaw this top-secret work known as the Manhattan Project. During his interview with Wouk, the physicist asked the novelist if he knew calculus. Wouk admitted that he did not. Feynman rejoined, "You had better learn it. It's the language God talks" (Strogatz 2019, vii).

It makes sense that a Nobel Prize winning physicist thinks God communicates through calculus. My instincts posit a different divine language: music. It is a view shared by many, going back to the ancient Greeks, who perceived the intimate relationship between mathematics and music. The philosopher Pythagoras and his followers believed that the stars and the planets existed in a cosmos that was harmonically ordered. They called this galactic symphony the "music of the spheres," an idea resurrected and further developed by the seventeenth-century astronomer Johannes Kepler in his *Harmonices Mundi*. Mixing science and theology, this publication claimed that the planets, including the earth, were subsumed into an astrological harmony. While most scientists today are disinclined to agree with Kepler's cosmic harmonics, some composers and even theologians concur that music is the stuff of sacred speech. A powerful summary of this view is placed on the lips of legendary composer Ludwig van Beethoven, who in a fictionalized film about his life, says:

> The vibrations on the air are the breath of God speaking to man's soul. Music is the language of God. We musicians are as close to God as man can be. We hear his voice, we read his lips, we give birth to the children of God, who sing his praise. That's what musicians are. (*Copying Beethoven* 2006)

In the previous chapter, we noted the pervasiveness of auditory images in Judeo-Christian revelation. Sonic communication appears to be a natural medium for the God of both the Old and New Testaments. It is also a crucial art form in religious rituals and Roman Catholic liturgy. Some might be surprised to learn that the *Constitution on the Sacred Liturgy* from the Second Vatican Council asserts that music is integral to our worship (112), a claim made for no other art form. Part of this power comes from music's ability to expand the meaning of a text and heighten its emotional content.

While music is most prized in Christian theology and liturgy for its ability to be wedded with words—especially the Word of God—it also has theological resonance beyond this logogenic function (meaning that the words take precedence over the melody, from Greek *logos* or "word"). It is also the very nature of sound that it amplifies the spiritual, even sacramental, aspects of music. For example, different from sculpture or painting, music vanishes when the song is completed or the etude is played. This produces a perceptible dynamic in music, which is more transitory than a fresco or other plastic art that endures long after the creative process is finished. Music occurs in the now. Some philosophers contend that music actually makes time audible. Sound also has a definite intangibility about it, different from the paint or paper or stone that is the stuff of other artisans. Furthermore, its capacity for human engagement is built into the human anatomy. While we have eyelids to block out sight, we have no "earlids" to close off sound. This physiological feature spurred theologian Karl Rahner to imagine human beings as primarily "hearers of the Word." Finally, there is clear evidence that the human imagination posits sound as an indicator of presence. That door creaking during a windstorm prompts us to ask with suspicion or alarm "Who's there?" These acoustic traits—

Luke 23:46. "Into your hands, I commend my Spirit."

For me this final dance in triple meter is appropriately tranquil and heroic because it symbolizes how every hope and need that unfolded in the preceding last words is forever resolved in Trinitarian Love. So those who condemned and crucified the holy one were forgiven before they asked. The eleventh-hour promise to thieves was honored. The gift of Mary as Mother to believers was ratified in her Golgothan adoption of the beloved disciple. The fear of abandonment by God in our darkest hour was washed away by blood and water. And every thirst for dignity and justice was quenched in this sacrificial gift.

Jesus could execute this final capitulation not in desperation but tranquility, because in his divinity he perceived that the whole of his life and mission—evoked in these seven final epitaphs—was taken up into the very dance of God. The ancient Greek Fathers, deft theologians in mystery, actually envisioned the Trinity as engaged in an eternal dance, a perichoresis: a divine minuet of the three in one. May the promise of this vision underscored by Papa Haydn's lyricism invite us in this penultimate moment before Easter to rehearse wholeheartedly and with unwavering hope the inevitable *consumatum est*—the "it is finished"—in our own lives. We embrace Haydn's musical mysticism so that we too, now and at the hour of our death, can freely and willingly enter into the dance of the Trinity when it is our turn to say "Father, into your hands I commend my spirit."

Except from Holy Week reflection on Haydn's *Seven Last Words* marked by impermanence, dynamism, intangibility, and the specter of presence—render it a particularly potent medium when communicating about or with a God perceived as dynamic, intangible, present, and residing in the eternal now. Because music contains no definitions —no one to date has been able to construct a sonic dictionary that explains its meanings—it remains a fundamentally ambiguous medium. Thus, it is well suited for the spiritual and is itself a form of "sound theology," appropriate for humans in our attempts to broach the divine.

A good friend who is a gifted violist recently gathered three other string players to perform Franz Joseph Haydn's *Seven Last Words of Christ* during Holy Week. Originally written for orchestra, the work was subsequently adapted for string quartet by the composer, who also produced an oratorio version for solo voices and chorus. My friend thought the string quartet version would be more appropriate for a Holy Week event, believing that the instrumental performance would invite a richer mode of contemplation than the choral rendering. To spark such introspection throughout the performance, seven speakers were invited to offer short reflections before each of the sections.

My reflection preceded the last of the seven words, "Into your hands, Lord, I commend my spirit." In studying the music—and not simply its textual inspiration (Luke 23:46)—I was astonished to discover that this instrumental reflection on Jesus' last words on the cross was not a sad and solemn composition cast in some melancholy minor key. Rather, it is a minuet, literally dance music, a courtly promenade announced in heroic E-flat major, a key employed by innumerable classical composers to represent the gallant and courageous. This inspired me to consider Haydn not only a monumental composer but literally a sound theologian. By imaginatively plying his compositional art in the service of spirituality, he opened for me new ways of pondering the terrible beauty of the sacrifice at the center of our Christian faith. I had never considered the process of dying as a dance with God, a holy promenade resolved in the harmony of Jesus' own dying and rising. Haydn's music created a new spiritual resonance that invited me and, I hope, those who heard my words to move deeper into the paschal mystery.

Of Poetry and Inclusivity

Poets, like other creative souls, can sometimes appear to be discon-nected from our reality. Fascinated by the wings of a dragonfly or dis-tracted by call of the loon, they can momentarily overlook what we might consider obvious. This penchant for distraction is whimsically illustrated by a tale of Sherlock Holmes and his sidekick, Dr. Watson. The two embarked upon a camping trip together. As they lay down for the night, Holmes says, "Watson, look up into the sky and tell me what you see." Watson replies, "I see millions and millions of stars." Holmes then asked, "And what does that tell you?" Watson replies, "Astronomi-cally, it tells me that there are millions of galaxies and potentially bil-lions of planets. Theologically, it tells me that God is great and that we are small and insignificant. Meteorologically, it tells me that we will have a beautiful day tomorrow. And what does it tell you, Sherlock?" Holmes coolly responds, "It tells me that somebody has stolen our tent."

Holmes' lyricism might not be helpful if we were tasked with craft-ing a user's guide for working a chainsaw ("Shake hands firmly but respectfully with this daunting new friend . . .") or asked to provide directions to the nearest hospital ("Find the lonely sycamore keeping watch over the landscape and turn left toward the beckoning sun . . ."). However, since preachers deal with matters spiritual and mysterious, the ruminations of poets are infinitely more useful to us than technical guides or a GPS device. Poets can teach us much about negotiating a gracious path through life's questions and shaping language for our assemblies to aid them as they do the same.

Language is notoriously ambiguous. Prominent linguists, such as Noam Chomsky, have argued that human speech is quite poorly designed for communication. Chomsky theorizes that language did not evolve for communication but for other reasons, such as a way to organize our own thoughts rather than share them with others. While this position is hotly debated among linguists and evolutionary biologists, no one questions that our words can be interpreted in wildly different ways. By nature, human speech is cryptic, opaque, vague, and sometimes even unintelligible.

While the porous character of language might sometimes be a gigantic obstacle for preachers, it is more often a blessing in disguise. As already noted, our homilizing is not an exercise in instruction but God's invitation to a relationship through our words. Flawed phrases and imperfect speech are the tools at hand for shaping a sacred bridge between the human and the holy. These auditory sacraments require all of the elasticity and ambiguity that language can muster to spark the religious imaginations and engage the profound questions of the baptized in all their diversity. Just as Jesus caught the attention of the people of his time through disruptive parable talk, so poets model how we can dismantle bland speech sufficiently that God's own unruly Spirit might break through.

Marie Howe is a former poet laureate of the state of New York. Her poetry has been described by her teacher and fellow poet Stanley Kunitz as lines that "address the mysteries of flesh and spirit, in terms accessible only to a woman who is very much of our time and yet still in touch with the sacred." In her unsettling work "The Star Market," Howe poetically disassembles the local grocery store, transforming it from a bland place of commerce into one filled with the unlikely people that Jesus loved. Her deconstruction plays well against the last judgment scenarios that populate the beginning and end of each liturgical year. Matthew's Gospel, for example, could be blithely heard as an antiseptic invitation to donate clothes or foodstuffs to a local pantry as a way to satisfy the scriptural injunction. Howe's craft uncomfortably closes the gap between the disciple and the stranger, between the sheep and goats, between the saint and the sinner. Her text places us at each other's elbows, so close that we become the other, recognize ourselves in the stranger, and find Jesus' imperative to love invading our very personal space.

One of the downsides of the design of our current lectionary is that we hear certain texts or their parallels with great regularity. Scriptural repetition can lead to scriptural domestication: the "ho-hum, heard that before, know what it means" syndrome. Poetry is an acute form of paying attention that splays open a familiar text, turns a domesticated lectionary reading inside out, and freshly disarms us against a divine Spirit that we think we can keep at bay.

Matthew 25:31–45. "As often as you did it for one of my least brothers, you did it for me."

As the poet muses:

The people Jesus loved were shopping at The Star Market yesterday.
An old lead-colored man standing next to me at the checkout
breathed so heavily I had to step back a few steps.

Even after his bags were packed he still stood, breathing hard and
hawking into his hand. The feeble, the lame, I could hardly look at them:
shuffling through the aisles, they smelled of decay, as if The Star Market

had declared a day off for the able-bodied, and I had wandered in
with the rest of them: sour milk, bad meat:
looking for cereal and spring water.

Jesus must have been a saint, I said to myself, looking for my lost car
in the parking lot later, stumbling among the people who would have
been lowered into rooms by ropes, who would have crept

out of caves or crawled from the corners of public baths on their hands
and knees begging for mercy.

If I touch only the hem of his garment, one woman thought,
    I will be healed.
Could I bear the look on his face when he wheels around?
    (Marie Howe, 15)

Of course Jesus always wheels around and looks at us, through the face of the stranger . . . so many strangers. And we feel paralyzed: what to do with so much hunger and homelessness? Am I absolved because the need is so overwhelming?

There is a legend about St. Augustine walking along the seashore where thousands of starfish had washed up on the beach. One little girl was furiously running back and forth, throwing one little starfish after another back into the water. The kindly saint said, "There are just too many to save; it really won't make a difference." The little girl never stopped running as she turned to the saint and said, "It will make a difference to this one," as she tossed it into the sea.

Every time we reach out it makes a difference, no matter how small our reach, no matter how feeble our gesture. But when we reach out together, gesture as one to the hungry, homeless, disrespected, and vulnerable, God's reign opens further and Christ's presence becomes more tangible to the world desperate for his healing.

Homily excerpt, Solemnity of Christ the King, Year A

Hidden Meaning and Sleep Giants

By beginning this chapter with a consideration of movies rather than novels, it might seem that I have dug myself into a small preaching hole. Employing film to illustrate the concept of artistic simulation and touting cinema as the most accessible and effective medium for such flights of fancy could seriously undercut any promotion of thoughtful fiction as a reliable preaching partner. Why read novels when you can see a movie? Or, maybe more problematic, why read a novel when it has been made into a movie?

Without retreating from my previous claim about the power of film, the emergence of motion pictures as a global economic and entertainment phenomenon does not diminish the power of history, poetry, memoirs, or fiction. In sheer numbers the volume of books published around the world each year dwarfs the number of films released. UNESCO, the United Nations Educational, Scientific, and Cultural Organization, calculates that over two million new book titles are published globally each year. Beyond the issue of scale, the great writing that consistently rises from this massive output often provides deeper immersion experiences than a movie can ever achieve.

Timothy Ferris, an American science writer, offers a useful perspective on this topic when he writes about the "sadness of maps." This sadness or imperfection occurs because maps contain less information than the territory they are trying to represent. Further, since maps ordinarily reduce a three-dimensional reality into two dimensions, they must distort the original data (Ferris 2005, 70–71). Similarly, when a book is transformed into a film, much has to be cut, reduced, reinterpreted, and at least partially distorted. Character development is by necessity curtailed, enriching subplots eliminated, and telling details about states of mind or other psychological factors erased. While visual effects and a musical score can make up for some of these omissions, they do not make the same demands upon our imaginations as a novel does.

Canadian philosopher Marshall McLuhan distinguished between what he considered "hot" and "cool" media. He contended that movies are a "hot" medium, whose enhanced visuals and soundtrack provide so much stimulation to the consumer that they do not need to exert much effort to fill in any details. The filmmaker does that for them. In contrast, McLuhan considered the printed word a cooler medium, requiring more engagement on the part of the reader for filling in the blanks, extracting value, and creating meaning through the reading process (McLuhan 1964, 22). Immersing ourselves in well-crafted fiction is an invitation to expand our creative mind. Besides enriching our vocabularies and providing inventive illustrations for the preaching endeavor, it also develops capacities for drinking deeply of texts. We can bring such learning to the lectionary selections and other liturgical propers, such as the collects and eucharistic prayers that weekly feed our preaching.

The Buried Giant is a lengthy and complex novel by the British author and Nobel Prize winner Kazuo Ishiguro. It is a fantasy set in Britain after the time of the legendary King Arthur. Since the time of Arthur, Britons and Saxons had lived together in peace, even though the king had overseen the slaughter of many Saxons and the burning of their villages. The peace has been maintained through the breath of an

---

Luke 21:5–19. "The day will come when not one stone will be left on another, but it will all be torn down."

Recently I finished reading *The Buried Giant*, a dark and brooding novel by Kazuo Ishiguro. At the center of the novel set in post–Arthurian England is the aging dragon Querig, whom Merlin enchanted. Querig's breath induces societal amnesia, dampening the memories of hatred and slaughter that grew out of Arthur's bloody conquest of the Saxons. And so there was a Camelot of sorts, but more a Camelotic ruse. And once the dragon was slain, memory returns, raising its fiendish head, promising only division and chaos.

Significant sections of the United States' population and the media seriously misjudged the degree of unrest and anger in our electorate. The election this past week did not create the unrest or division. Rather, like the slaying of Querig, it erased some amnesiac fog and exposed us in stark but unmistaken ways as anything but the "United" States of America.

Today's apocalyptic readings could seem an appropriate commentary, announcing that calamity is near. But Jesus is not a prophet of doom. In Luke's Gospel, he is not simply foretelling temple destruction,

---

enchanted dragon. Merlin had cast a spell over the beast, and its breath descended as a memory-erasing mist. The betrayal of the Saxons by Arthur's men was forgotten, and a foggy harmony settled over the land. In the end, the last of the Arthurian knights who had protected the dragon for decades meets a powerful young Saxon in battle. The knight is defeated, the dragon slain, and the fog lifted. As memory returns, old hatreds stir and the lingering peace dissipates in the sun.

Preaching on the Sunday after the 2016 national election in the United States was traumatic for many, including me. The turmoil in the country, the disorientation in my own community of faith, and the dramatic polarization that was revealed in the electorate rendered the pulpit a very unappealing place to be that week. Quite frankly, I did not want to preach. Ishiguro's novel gave me a framework within which I could comment upon the post-election reality without being too partisan. It provided metaphors around memory, division, and enchantment that proved useful in the difficult homiletic task of that day. Ishiguro demonstrated for me again that fiction can be true, fantasy may hold a treasury of meaning, and myths are capable of leading us into holy mysteries.

Conclusion

A number of years ago the writers from the *Washington Post* designed a social experiment about paying attention, priorities, and preferences. One cold January morning, a young man in a baseball cap and a sweatshirt placed his open violin case on the floor of a Metro station in Washington, DC, and began to play Bach. It was rush hour, and during his forty-five-minute performance of recognized masterpieces, thousands of people passed through that station. Only six people stopped and lingered. About twenty commuters put money in the violin case but kept walking. After the forty-five-minute experiment, the musician had collected $32 in tips. As he finished there was no applause or recognition that Joshua Bell, one of the finest violinists of his generation, had just offered a free performance on his $3.5 million Stradivarius.

The article by Gene Weingarten narrating this event won a Pulitzer Prize. One observation in his reporting has received the most attention over the years. He wrote:

> There was no ethnic or demographic pattern to distinguish the people who stayed to watch Bell, or the ones who gave money, from that vast majority who hurried on past, unheeding. Whites, blacks and Asians, young and old, men and women, were represented in all three groups. But the behavior of one demographic remained absolutely consistent. Every single time a child walked past, he or she tried to stop and watch. And every single time, a parent scooted the kid away.

Jesus' admonition about the necessity to become like little children for entering God's reign (Matthew 18:3) comes to mind when I read Weingarten's story. As preachers, we bring to bear all of our learning, experience, wisdom, and spirituality when we set about to construct a homiletic bridge between people's lives and God's holy revelation. The arts remind us to bring our childlike imaginations and our openness to beauty wherever we may find it to this holy enterprise. It might enable a surprising number of folks to cross that bridge with more ease and even grace.

References

Chomsky, Noam. 2010. "Some Simple Evo-Devo Theses: How True Might They Be for Language?" In *Approaches to the Evolution of Language*. Ed. by Richard K. Larson, Vivian M. Deprez, and Hiroko Yamakido, 92–161. Cambridge: Cambridge University Press.

Copying Beethoven. 2006. Myriad Pictures.

Ferris, Timothy. 2005. *The Whole Shebang: A State-of-the-Universe(s) Report*. New York: Simon and Schuster.

Howe, Marie. 2008. *The Kingdom of Ordinary Time*. New York: W. W. Norton.

Jackson, Joe. 2016. *Black Elk: The Life of an American Visionary*. New York: Farrar, Straus and Giroux.

Kennedy, John. 1964. "The Purpose of Poetry." *Atlantic Monthly* 213, no. 2: 53–54.

McLuhan, Marshall. 1964. *Understanding Media: The Extensions of Man*. New York: McGraw Hill.

Mitchell, Nathan. 1996. "Amen Corner," *Worship* 70, no. 3: 251–260.

Revell, Donald. 2007. *The Art of Attention: A Poet's Eye*. St. Paul: Graywolf Press.

Strogatz, Steven. 2019. *Infinite Powers: How Calculus Reveals the Secrets of the Universe*. Boston: Houghton Mifflin Harcourt.

Tweedy, Damon. 2015. *Black Man in a White Coat: A Doctor's Reflections on Ease and Medicine*. New York: Picador.

Weingarten, Gene. 2014 "Pearls before Breakfast." *The Washington Post* (September 23, 2014).

CHAPTER 6

Some Assembly Required

If you're going to have a story, have a big story, or none at all.

~Joseph Campbell

A favorite Christmas story from my family's folklore, appropriately embellished over the decades, centers on the wishes of a younger sister to have Santa Claus bring her a Barbie Dreamhouse. While of limited means, my parents struggled mightily to make each Christmas memorable, attempting to fulfill and often anticipate the usually modest wishes of their children. That year they located my sister's desired gift in one of those enormous catalogues that appeared on our doorstep each autumn. Weeks later Dad dutifully drove to Sears & Roebuck to pick up the treasure. I was of a post–Santa Claus age at the time, and I was in on the plot. I remember Dad bringing in a large, flat box, which he and Mom hid under the bed in the inner sanctum of their bedroom, safe from the prying eyes of inquisitive children. Since Santa Claus only showed up at our house when believers were asleep on Christmas Eve, my parents hauled out the box after my younger siblings were tucked away. While Dad presumed that the dollhouse would need to be assembled, neither he nor Mom were prepared for the byzantine directions and hundreds of maneuvers necessary for constructing this highly anticipated gift. Made of heavy cardboard, the pieces were to be fitted together according to a tab-and-slot design. Mom read out the directions, while Dad, an industrial engineer, would try to figure out where "tab G" was, and how it fit into "slot G." They labored into the wee hours in mounting frustration, desperate to finish this cardboard castle before my younger siblings would bolt out of their rooms at the crack of dawn. To this day, the phrase "some assembly required" strikes fear into the hearts of many of my family members (Foley 2015, 91–92).

The previous pages of this book have provided resources for aiding preachers in pursuing the task critical to our preaching ministry: theological reflection. To this end, the insistent call to pay attention prods us to wonder, "Where is God, and what is the good news in this joyous or lamentable moment of our individual and shared lives?" That question, the bedrock of our baptismal vocation, gives rise to a second one for those of us who preach: "How can I enable those who hear the Word proclaimed recognize this holy and wholly pervasive presence in their lives, individually and communally?" To that end, we delved into fields such as pastoral ethnology to aid us in the deep listening essential for respecting believers and the environments that both honor and overwhelm them. We revisited the elements of the liturgical landscape to unearth their richness for authentic liturgical preaching. We ventured into the world of the natural and social sciences to ponder the wonder they evoke and the perspective they provide about the sacramentality of the cosmos. Then we turned to the universe where arts and artists of every kind stimulate our thoughts and emotions, potentially firing the homiletic soul.

Throughout these ventures, we have tried to model how these resources might be fruitfully engaged and respectfully exploited in service of the Word. These pages have been punctuated with poetic references, insights from the sciences, literary allusions, and borrowings from popular culture. This selective modeling is no recipe to be followed, and each preacher needs to craft a message for their particular congregation, in its social and religious context, at a specific moment in time, and in harmony with their own gifts and experiences. Each homily is an act of constructive theology that cannot be achieved by employing some prepackaged sermon or theoretical design. It is very clear that more than "some assembly" is required here.

While homily composition is no tab-and-slot exercise—insert Gospel A into Assembly B—there are some overarching strategies that could contribute to the effectiveness of constructing these works of local theology. There are four in particular that I have found personally effective and that esteemed preachers and other sources affirm as consistently beneficial for the art of homily crafting: storytelling, language and rhetoric, problematizing the texts, and performative skills.

Storytelling: The Narrative Advantage

We humans keep trying to discover what differentiates us from other species. Tool usage was long a favorite example of our difference until primatologists demonstrated that chimpanzees, among other species, were quite adept at shaping and employing utensils to acquire food or fend off enemies. Language won the day for centuries until scientists began to produce data confirming that highly intelligent species such as dolphins also had sophisticated forms of communication. There is one cultural artifact, however, known to virtually every human civilization and as yet undocumented in the animal world that seems to set us apart: the art of storytelling. In his fascinating exploration of the narrative gift, *The Storytelling Animal*, Jonathan Gottschall contends that we are not only *homo sapiens,* or wise people, but also *homo fictus,* storytelling animals.

Human history itself is a storytelling adventure. Cave paintings from over forty thousand years ago seem to depict idealized tales of hunts, while ancient forms of some fairy tales could date back to the Ice Age. Religion is not immune from this storytelling instinct. Many commentators have remarked about the narrative quality of local and global religions and their scriptures. Decades ago, the respected biblical scholar Amos Wilder asserted that among the many literary forms present in the Old Testament, the narrative mode was primary (Wilder 1969, 51). The design of the Book of Genesis hints that the Holy One must have been the aboriginal storyteller; we could not possibly have known of these stories without the divine narrator enlightening us. The God of the Hebrew Scriptures is indeed *Deus fictus,* a storytelling God. More than half of the Old Testament consists of narration; the Gospels and the Acts of the Apostles contain even a higher concentration of stories. Jesus is clearly portrayed as a master storyteller, especially gifted in the art of the parable. Wilder concludes that Christian communication itself is ordinarily achieved through story.

Multiple hypotheses are proposed to explain why this penchant for narrative is so rampant across our species. Some scientists contend that the human brain is actually wired for storytelling. This approach argues that our storytelling capacity developed as a form of defense against the chaos of data that bombards us. To avoid sensory overload, our brains developed the capacity to create stories as a way to package experience into a portable and pliable format. In addition to serving as a kind of storage bin for information, the tales we weave help us make sense of the world. This interpretive function is related to the image of simulation discussed in the last chapter. Cognitive scientist Keith Oatley argues that storytelling is a way to test out responses to difficult situations without much danger.

Further, psychologist Dan McAdams and others believe that storytelling is crucial for forging a coherent image of ourselves and that it is a uniquely human mode not only for expressing but also creating ourselves and our world. This is the process of shaping what he calls a "narrative identity." McAdams believes this is a particularly critical task for those passing from adolescence into young adulthood. Social scientists have recently concluded that these eighteen to twenty-seven-year-olds constitute a unique demographic, called "emerging adults." During this crucial period of development, these individuals need to craft broad and self-defining life narratives that can support and nourish their existence with some semblance of unity, purpose, and meaning (McAdams 2013, 246).

> [Fiction] is a particularly useful simulation because negotiating the social world effectively is extremely tricky, requiring us to weigh up myriad interacting instances of cause and effect. Just as computer simulations can help us get to grips with complex problems such as flying a plane or forecasting the weather, so novels, stories and dramas can help us understand the complexities of social life.
>
> Keith Oatley

One particular finding about storytelling is worth noting here. In chapter 1 we stressed the importance of empathy in those who exercise a preaching ministry. It is an essential capacity for homilists who wish to create the kind of pastoral and spiritual engagement that renders our preaching effective. Neuroscientists and others believe they can establish a link between fiction and our empathetic instincts. Keith Oatley is one who argues that narrative allows us to map the way other people think and believe. It improves the previously discussed capacity known as "theory of mind" and the ability to distinguish another's feelings or commitments from our own. Although it might seem hard to believe, experiments also seem to prove that effective storytelling activates certain biochemical reactions in the brain that increase not only empathy but also a spirit of generosity. The Roman Catholic philosopher Richard Kearney summarizes this by noting that an empathetic imagination is a narrative imagination. He concludes, "If we possess narrative sympathy—enabling us to see the world from the other's point of view—we cannot kill. If we do not, we cannot love" (Kearney 2002, 140).

These scientific findings provide fresh impetus for doing what preachers have done from time immemorial: we have told stories. While doctrinal lectures, moralizing discourses, and catechetical sessions have too often displaced homilizing, storytelling has remained a time-tested device for engaging the baptized and breaking open the Word. This preaching instinct found new momentum at the end of the twentieth century in what is sometimes called the "narrative turn" in homiletics. Besides Amos Wilder, preachers such as Fred Craddock, Richard Jensen, and Eugene Lowry were pioneers in this more inductive method, which placed the hearer rather than the preacher at the center of the sermon. In this turn, storytelling became virtually indispensable.

My own preaching preparation involves untold hours searching out and compiling narratives that prompt images of empathy and generosity. These are virtues foundational for fulfilling the great commandment to love our neighbors, and not just those who look or think like us. Especially valuable are stories with a parabolic quality about them, upending our expectations and confronting us with that kind of raw revelation Jesus so often summoned. This is not narrative entertainment but a powerful unveiling that startles complacent hearts and provides new pathways for God's own Spirit. A few years ago, I found one such story by Leslie Guttman about her encounter with an unexpected stranger in a bookstore. (See next page.) It provided me with a new lens for interpreting Jesus' encounter with the Samaritan woman in John 4. The pathos in the tale helped me imagine why Jesus stayed so long in the Samaritan village. It also made me reimagine the gifts that the woman who met Jesus at Jacob's well might have brought to the table. It

John 4:5–42. Jesus had to pass through Samaria.

"The bookstore was packed. A woman with long, black hair about five feet away was leafing through [a book]. I glanced up in time to see her slip a book into her satchel and walk off. I hesitated and then walked after her. 'Pssst,' I said, pointing at the satchel. Up close, I saw that she was about thirty, probably homeless. Her khaki parka was filthy, her hair matted. The satchel was bursting with her belongings. She gave me a sorrowful look handed me the book and ran off. The book was a journal designed for someone who was grieving. Someone like me. It was beautifully bound, the paper creamy and heavy. It had space to write the answers to statements like: "It's hard for me to be without you when I . . .'' 'She's been wanting that book,' said the manager who watched the whole thing. 'She comes in all the time and looks at it. Sometimes, she puts it on hold, but then she never gets it.'

"Dammit! Why did I have to be such a Goody Twoshoes? Why didn't I just let her steal it? I ran out of the store and caught up with her a block away. 'Did you just lose someone?' I said. 'My grandmother,' she [replied.] 'I miss her so much I can't stand it.' I told her about my stepdad, who had just passed away. His kindness had knit our family together for eighteen years. I handed her the book, we both stood on the curb and wept. " (Guttman, 2011)

For the first time since my stepdad died, I felt understood—as only a stranger can understand you, without inadequacy or regret. Up until then, I had felt alone in my grief, reluctant to turn to my family because they were grieving, too. This encounter made me want to stay open to the chance meeting with an important stranger, the possibility of unplanned symmetry that is luminous and magical.

Unplanned symmetry: maybe that is what happened to Jesus in his encounter with the Samaritan woman. He was a source of living water to her, but in her openness and her fearless words about him to others of her village she returned the gift, affirming that he was on the right path even though it would cost him his life.

Living in a world where strangers abound, lepers lurk, and Samaritans wait around every corner is dangerous. But this is where Jesus calls us to live out our baptism, in luminous and unplanned symmetry, in chance encounters with the other, knowing we are not alone on that journey, but always accompanied by God's sustaining Spirit.

Homily excerpt, Third Sunday of Lent, Year A.

is traditional to announce that Jesus brought salvation and new life to her and her community. This fresh parable sparked a growing comprehension that she in turn might have also brought a particular gift to him, important for his ministerial journey.

Language and Rhetoric: Persuasive Words

We can imagine our homiletic endeavors in a myriad of ways. We might consider it a form of revelation and a freshly contextualized sounding of God's Word. Some conceptualize their preaching in a more missionary mode, as a kind of spiritual call to arms for the baptized to labor more vigorously for the inbreaking of God's kingdom of justice and peace. Then there is the time-honored purpose of inviting hearers to a more intimate relationship with the Holy One, rooted in deep piety and faithfulness.

Whether cued to revelation, mission, or intimacy, however, the preaching enterprise can rightly be envisioned as an exercise in persuasion. While we might not always be forthcoming about our motives, or even aware of them, we craft our language and shape our message to influence the thinking, believing, and acting of our hearers. By evoking dogma and drilling down on Church teaching during a homily, for example, we are implicitly attempting to persuade them of the authority and moral credibility of the Church. When we tenderly unpack an encounter between Jesus and widows or lepers or children, we are prompting assemblies to acknowledge a sacred heart at the center of our believing and accept the invitation to develop one as well. When we engage the Church's teaching on social justice and the preferential option for the poor, we are spurring the baptized toward a vision of Church less focused on self-maintenance and more outwardly directed in how it directs its energies.

Admittedly, casting our preaching as an exercise in persuasion could make us feel a bit uneasy and prompt us to ask, "Where is the Holy Spirit in all of this?" For centuries there has existed a deviant theological tendency to believe that we humans can achieve our own salvation or do so for others. The fifth-century theologian Pelagius in particular was accused of denying the need for God's assistance in doing good and of contending that our gift of free will naturally disposed us for achieving holiness.

I am not proposing that preachers can move people to moral righteousness or sanctity simply through their personal rhetorical skills. It is God's saving Spirit that graces us with faith, and that same Spirit who accompanies us into a life of virtue. However, preachers, like other ministers, are prized instruments for this holy bestowal. As previously noted, St. Paul wondered how someone can believe unless another preaches (Romans 10:14). Effective preachers are called to be channels of grace and hope for God's people, instruments of fostering and nourishing faith. Language is the essential tool for this work. Homilizing is a speech-act, and the way we deploy our words affects the baptized's capacity for receiving God's Word. While we rely on the Spirit of God to move our hearers to faith, we must also continue to develop our skills as speakers to persuade them to be open to that Spirit. Preachers and other public speakers are helped by the modes of persuasion, or rhetorical appeals, that Aristotle described: *ethos, pathos,* and *logos.*

Ethos

To be blunt, rhetoric is sometimes distrusted as fancy talk or verbal trickery that can distract people from the truth. How often we have seen an over-the-top infomercial with some smooth talking salesman—or even a preacher—that seems to confirm that rhetoric is a skill for deception. In classical understandings, however, the credibility of the speaker is integral to the rhetorical arts. This is often referenced as *ethos,* a Greek word appropriately translated here as "character."

Ancient commentators on the topic, such as Aristotle, understood *ethos* as the trust listeners place in the speaker's personal character and knowledge. Such trust is established even before the speaking event—for example, by the quality of pastoral care that preachers provide to their community beyond the sanctuary. Creating an *ethos* of trustworthiness also occurs in the midst of our preaching. We persuade our listeners to depend on us in the homiletic moment because we demonstrate ourselves to be knowledgeable about the topic and about the community. Without providing verbal footnotes or quoting learned tomes as though we were offering an academic lecture, our reflective work and prayerful study become transparent in our preaching, as does their lack. Preparation is critical to preaching, especially so for those who preach to the same assembly season after season. They know our stories and our styles, our go-to authorities and trusted documents. In our sustained ministry with them, establishing a credible *ethos* in our preaching is never a completed task, but something we renew each time we venture into the ambo.

Pathos

Besides cultivating the art of *ethos,* a second aspect of our speaking intimately related to its persuasive power is what the Greeks called *pathos*. Similar to its usage in English, the ancients used this term to speak of suffering but also more generally of experience. In a rhetorical sense, *pathos* is the power to move an audience or assembly to a desired emotional state that will compel them to act in accord with the speaker's wishes. It is this aspect of oratory, more than others, that has the potential for social and political manipulation.

Even so, *pathos* is a critical aspect of effective homilizing. The pioneering work of theologian Don Saliers on the relationship between liturgy and ethics is most instructive for our purpose. According to Saliers, affect or emotion plays a central role in this relationship. These are not fleeting feelings but deep passions and the accompanying virtues that develop and emerge over time. Our worship is replete with what Saliers calls "Christian affections." How often in the celebration of Eucharist do we sing and pray about contrition and blessedness, thanksgiving and peace, gratitude and remorse. Similarly, Pope Francis' approach to evangelization is his amplification of the role of joy at the heart of this mission. This profound affection was the very gift that Jesus offered to his disciplines during his farewell discourse at the Last Supper. This deep emotion was not for its own sake, but in service to the command that we are to love one another (John 15:11–12). Similarly, Saliers contends that our public worship is morally effective to the extent that our Christian affections and virtues are formed and expressed in our shared ritual actions (Saliers 1994).

A piece of wisdom from the African American community is that there can be no fire in the pews if there is ice in the pulpit. The poet Mary Oliver notes that attention without feeling is only a report. Preachers are not reporters but emissaries of salvific news. The pulpit is no more a venue for venting personal displeasures or good fortune than it is a place for promoting personal politics. It is, however, a premiere platform for rehearsing our passion for the Gospel, our thirst for justice, and our delight in God's eternal Word.

Logos

The third leg of the rhetorical tripod set out by Aristotle and other classical writers is *logos*. This is a Greek word more familiar to us; the beginning of John's Gospel dramatically announces Jesus as the very *Logos* or Word of God. In classical rhetoric, however, *logos* is more about how an argument is structured and the logic of its content. Some translate *logos* in this situation as "text." There are as many ways to structure a homily as there are homilists. Great teachers of preaching often provide clear designs for shaping a sermon that can be especially useful to beginners. While there is one useful structural technique that I will explore below—that is, developing the "oops" in the texts—I do not promote one compositional design over another. Rather, my emphasis is on specifics forms of speech that seem to possess unique powers to engage and persuade. Particularly important here are metaphorical and sensory language.

Deep in our memories there may lurk warnings from teachers of English composition and even speech instructors to avoid purple prose: those flowery and overwrought passages that draw attention to themselves while contributing little to a story line or argument. Such composition is so appalling that San Jose State University actually awards a purple-prose award every year for the worst opening sentence to the worst possible novel. The inspiration was the infamous first line of Edward Bulwer-Lytton's novel *Paul Clifford*: "It was a dark and stormy night." In reaction to this purple prose approach, some revert to other rhetorical extreme sometimes known the "*Dragnet* syndrome." This police drama portrayed the systematic nature of law enforcement. Its most famous cliché was repeated by the lead detective, Sergeant Joe Friday. Often, to refocus a rambling witnesses, Sergeant Friday said, "Just the facts, ma'am. Just the facts."

Preachers need to negotiate with care the linguistic space between "It was a dark and stormy night" and "Just the facts, ma'am." Our language cannot be so flowery and obtuse that the baptized get lost in a forest of modifiers. At the same time, we cannot forget that we are confronting mystery here. This is not simply the facts but the holy. The sciences might be a useful guide here in discerning the middle ground between Paul Clifford and Sergeant Joe Friday. This is particularly true when it comes to metaphorical language and vivid sensory imagery.

While poets have always understood that metaphors are powerful and memorable, neuroscientists are beginning to explain why. For example, researchers at Emory University discovered that the use of metaphors such as to "shoulder responsibility" or "twist my arm" activate regions

> Be careful of words
> Even the miraculous ones.
> For the miraculous we do our best.
> Sometimes they swarm like insects
> And leave not a sting but a kiss.
> They can be as good as fingers.
> They can be as trusty as the rock
> You stick your bottom on.
> But they can be both daisies and bruises. . . .
>
> But I try to take care
> And be gentle to them.
> Words and eggs must be handled with care.
> Once broken they are impossible
> Things to repair.
>
> Anne Sexton, 71

of the brain important for sensing texture through touch. However, those regions were not triggered by literal phrases with the same meaning, such as "take responsibility" or "pay the bill" (Lacy 2017). This and other experiments demonstrate that metaphors connected with sensory and motor experiences actually have a biological impact on us. So much so, that some researchers talk about the "metaphorical brain."

Similarly, when researchers in Spain asked participants to read words with strong odor associations, like *garlic,* the part of the brain involved in the sense of smell lit up. In related work, French scientists found when participants read sentences like "Mary grasped the object" or "Pablo kicked the ball," there was noticeable activity in the part of the brain that coordinates the body's movement. It appears that the brain distinguishes little between reading or even hearing about an object or action and actually experiencing it in the flesh. Speech that deploys strong visual, emotional, or other sense imagery can trigger as many as seven different regions of the brain, whereas the transmission of data ordinarily engages only two of them. The effect of vibrant language in the art of persuasion is even acknowledged to affect our judicial system. As Sapolsky summarizes, "Every trial lawyer knows [that] juries decide differently depending on how colorfully you describe someone's act" (Sapolsky 2017, 93).

The words we choose make a difference in the persuasiveness of our speech and its effectiveness in inviting our hearers deeper into the mystery of God. Most of us are not particularly gifted orators, and constructing such language might not come naturally to us. Immersing ourselves in the homilies and other writings of those who have this skill deepens our awareness of such linguistic possibilities. Then comes our vocational task: the thoughtful shaping of our words week after week that they might be both accessible and evocative.

Problematizing the Texts: The Parable and the Oops

One of the most common narrative devices used in literature, film, and even video games is the plot twist. This literary technique does precisely what its name implies: it turns the story line in an unexpected direction, shocking and sometimes even upsetting the reader, viewer, or gamer. Storytellers have been employing this technique since at least the time of the ancient Greek dramatists. One classical example is the tragedy *Oedipus rex* by the Athenian playwright Sophocles. Oedipus fulfills a prophecy that he has attempted to escape his entire life: he kills his own father and then marries his mother. This form of plot reversal, which pivots on the shocking recognition of a previously hidden identity, is the stuff of high drama and slapstick comedy. Sometimes it is handled deftly; sometimes it seems to be an act of desperation in hopes of saving a weak story line. Two celebrated media franchises relied on this technique for their dramatic unfolding. *Game of Thrones* stunned audiences when it was revealed late in the series that the character Jon Snow, thought to be the illegitimate child of Lord Ned Stark, was actually born of the royal house of Targaryen and was a rightful heir to the Iron Throne. Similarly, the final movie of the original *Star Wars* saga discloses that the last Jedi knight, Rey, is the granddaughter of the evil Emperor Palpatine.

While most preachers are not overly concerned about plot development and hidden identities, professional screen writers and playwrights exercise a kind of shrewdness that can serve our ministry. One accomplished homilist and teacher who has been especially attentive to their gifts is Eugene Lowry, an important promoter of the narrative turn in preaching. One of Lowry's key contributions was not only stressing that preaching is a storytelling genre, but also teaching how to construct a sermon so that the narrative has its greatest effect.

Lowry's central concern was that a sermon should have a plot or a compelling narrative, not simply some theological point. Too often sermons are shaped around ideas that unfold through a series of unrelated arguments or explanations. The implicit goal of such preaching is understanding. Preaching, however, is not essentially cognitive but relational, it is not about knowing but about transformation and mission. Lowry's approach capitalizes on the reality that life is not experienced as a series of propositions or even useful ideas. Rather, it occurs to us as events, processes, tension, and the struggle for resolution. That is why we instinctively relate our experiences as a narrative rather than as a series of abstract hypotheses to be proven or rejected. He summarizes:

> [A] sermon is not a doctrinal lecture. It is an event-in-time, a narrative art form more akin to a play or novel in shape than to a book. Hence we are not engineering scientists; we are narrative artists by professional function. . . . I propose that we begin by regarding the sermon as a homiletical plot, a narrative art form, a sacred story. (Lowry 2000, xx, xxi)

Related to this emphasis on preaching as sacred storytelling is a simple narrative strategy at once obvious but still too often hidden in plain sight: storytellers should not give away the plot too soon. Lowry explains:

> Unfortunately, we have been taught to begin our sermons by giving away the plot—even to include in the introduction a one-sentence abstract of sorts. As a result, we become homiletical equivalents to a foolish playwright going to center stage prior to the drama to announce the central points to be communicated by the drama. If such were to occur in the theater, the audience, having no further reason to stay, would have sufficient cause to get up and leave the theater. (Lowry 2000, 35–36)

Predictability in a story line allows tension to evaporate and interest to wane. That is certainly one reason why the creators of their respective franchises did not reveal the true identity of John Snow or Rey until very late in the series. If you know the ending already, why trudge on through the story?

Eugene Lowry has crafted a unique strategy for designing a homily that progresses through five stages. I do not advocate imitating the preaching style of any particular homilist, nor do I promote any particular way to structure a homily. There is, however, one compelling element in Lowry's process that I do favor in my own preaching and recommend wholeheartedly. He calls it "upsetting the equilibrium" or "uncovering the oops." This move, which Lowry places early in his sermon construction, is meant to introduce ambiguity in the listeners and prod them to journey with the preacher in confronting and resolving that ambiguity.

The Spanish philosopher José Ortega y Gasset once noted, "It's good to aggravate people a little. It makes them pay attention." While upsetting the people of God is not a primary goal of our preaching, the reality is that God's Word is at least disconcerting if not disruptive. That is clearly revealed in the Incarnate Word, who upset the equilibrium of the pious of his day by preaching an inclusivity in word and deed that shocked his co-religionists. Parables by their very nature are plot-twisters, pulling the rug out from under the listeners' well-constructed worldview, and inviting them into the ambiguity of God's ways that are not our ways (Isaiah 55:8). Instead of calling it aggravation, Lowry uses the more visceral image of moving from itch to scratch. How can our homilies lift up some existential or spiritual itch that the assembly metaphorically needs to scratch?

While Barbara Brown Taylor characterizes herself as a "detective of divinity" (as previously noted), Lowry prompts us to be "detectives of dilemmas." Finding the "oops" means engaging those gnawing but often unspoken questions that befuddle and sometimes sadden believers in enduring ways. We do not need to invent these. They are the puzzles and mysteries that both define and sometimes deflate our humanity. Our skills in pastoral ethnography and care allow us to discern in them the unfolding mystery of God and the promise of a paschal resolution. Our empathy also allows us to reveal in modest ways that we too share these dilemmas, that we are not above the struggles of this world, and that we are committed companions with the baptized on the way toward their resolution in Jesus Christ.

As the mystery of God would have it, the writing of this chapter has coincided with the eruption of the COVID-19 pandemic and orders throughout the United States to "shelter in place." Churches are shuttered; in the state of Illinois, gatherings of more than ten people are forbidden, and only those businesses deemed essential are allowed to remain operating. In a matter of weeks, the unemployment rate has shot up from 4.4 percent to more than 20 percent and continues to rise. It is Holy Week, and a homily for the Easter Vigil looms on the horizon. One does not have to search very far for ambiguity or examples of heart-wrenching dilemma in the current climate. As a liturgical preacher, however, my challenge pushes me deeper. The homiletic task here is to discover how the worship itself reflects and maybe even embodies such ambiguity and dilemma and, in turn, how it points a path out of this unimagined predicament.

My tack is to play on the paradox of the Easter Vigil itself, which weaves together darkness with light, the quarantine of the tomb with liberation, and death with life. A powerful ally in this endeavor is the *Exsultet*, which served as the opening ritual in this abbreviated liturgy, which was live-streamed while celebrated in an empty church. That ancient hymn does not shy away from embracing the darkness, with its recurring refrain, "This is the night." Rather, in tempered joy, the

Exsultet reminds us of an often overlooked mystery: Resurrection is birth in the blackness of night, through an immersion in the darkness of the grave, so that tomb can transform to womb, and an eternal light might break upon us. Jesus could linger in the tomb for three days because God's spirit was there, waiting in the darkness, preparing to incubate the Jesus of history into the Cosmic Christ. Darkness is not our enemy, Lent is not to be shunned, the cross is not to be forgotten, and even the ultimate quarantine of the grave is not hopeless.

The equilibrium of life is frequently unsettled, in both small and unfathomable ways. Jesus was the unsettling of Israel, and the parable of his living and dying summons believers into the intimacy of God in all of its uncertainty and promise. That is the mystery we are called to preach in all of its angst and ambiguity. Therein lie the unfolding promises of God.

Performative Skills: Abandoning the "Think System"

When preparing a homily or writing an article or a book it is useful to avoid unnecessary repetition of examples, stories, and language. Aware of that caution, I return to the charming swindler Professor Harold Hill who bamboozles the inhabitants of River City in the Broadway classic *The Music Man,* already discussed in chapter 3. Professor Hill offers a pointed warning about our homily preparation. Hill poses as a bandleader, announcing his intention to form a boys' band so he can sell instruments and uniforms to the parents of young boys. He has no music training and plans to skip town once he has pocketed the money. When questioned about his instructional methods, Hill comments, "You don't have to bother with the notes." Instead, he advocates the "think system," which requires no practicing on an actual instrument. Rather, all the preparation takes place in the head.

The method for developing homilies imparted to me and so many others in our formative years could be characterized as a "think" method. While compelled to be up on our feet from time to time in preaching courses, the actual performance of the homily was seldom if ever an integral element of the preparation process. Rather, that was largely a spiritual-exegetical-compositional undertaking. We prayed through texts, studied commentaries and other sources, and then designed the sermon either as an outline or a fully written document. The first time our words were performed was ordinarily when we moved to the ambo and delivered them during worship.

Like ballet or rap, preaching is a performative art requiring skilled enactment and nuanced delivery. Singers not only warm up before performing, they rehearse their music intensely, often committing it to memory. Professional dancers similarly expend endless hours getting various routines into their bodies and not simply into their heads. Preaching is an embodied act as well. The process of sound transmission and vocalization does not simply take place in the head. It is a matter of breath, resonance, and projection. Singers do not make music only with their vocal chords; like actors, they employ the whole body as their first and primary instrument of communication. Preachers do as well.

Advocating the practices of professional singers or dancers or actors might seem counterintuitive for pondering the ministry of preaching. No one wants an actor or a song-and-dance man in the pulpit. Instead, our assemblies long for the authentic believer, the transparent minister, who journeys with honesty and integrity with the baptized into the divine mysteries. Ironically, being our most authentic public self takes practice. It is not uncommon for preachers to assume a different persona or to acquire a "preaching voice" when delivering a sermon. One colleague from middle America surprisingly develops a British accent when homilizing. Introverts in particular sometimes feel that they have to morph temporarily into an extrovert in the homiletic moment. I have seen this happen countless times through decades of students. Learning to be a "public introvert"—true to oneself, yet up to the admittedly risky demands of this ecclesial act—takes both practice and method.

Preaching, like presiding, is an art that requires discipline in the preparation and in the delivery. Discipline is not synonymous with rigidity. Yes, there is a place for spontaneity and improvisation in the delivery. As the professionals from Chicago's Second City comedy club to the jazz greats of New Orleans remind us, improvisation is not simply making something up on the spot. It is a craft that requires preparation and cultivation. As a young organ student, I once was allowed to sit quietly in the nave of a church while one of the most celebrated organists of the day was rehearsing for an evening recital on the massive four-manual organ in the loft. Renowned for his improvisatory skills, the highlight of the evening was to be his creating of a fugue based on a theme that would be presented to him at the end of the concert. He would then extemporize the finale right before our eyes. As I listened to him rehearse, I could hear the maestro's assistant giving him sixteen-note theme after sixteen-note theme, each of which the organist would develop into a full-blown fugue. This went on for over an hour. He was practicing the art of improvisation.

Few if any of us have personal assistants to aid us in our homily prep. However, many of us do have smartphones and computers with built-in recording capacities. Performing our homilies into these substitute assemblies has multiple advantages. First, it provides us with a safe, non-judgmental environment for hearing how we sound when preaching. Listening to the delivery allows us to consider the amount of tonal interest, vocal variation, and interpretive savvy we bring to the text. Stunning theologizing delivered in a flat monotone may not be enough to pry people away from their own phone or from the parish bulletin. As a side benefit, recording our practice allows us to judge the length of our preaching. While I might predict that my homily will run nine minutes on a given Sunday, my phone may shock me with a different verdict: 13 minutes and 20 seconds. Maybe a little surgery on the text is necessary here.

How dramatically to deliver the homily is a matter of both individual taste and cultural expectations. Preaching is an unusually personal and contextual mode of Christian witness. Our homilizing style should be attuned to our assemblies while yet resonating with our authentic selves. At the same time, however, inviting others to believe in a God so impassioned that nothing would restrain divinity from pursuing humanity—not even the death of the Only Begotten—presumes some fire in the pulpit. As Don Saliers notes, a valuable aspect of our theological reflection on preaching is examining to what extent our own fervor for God's Word, our passion for the Gospel, our zeal for the marginalized, and our affection for the baptized is palpable in our homilizing. Intention is useful, but in this performative ministry it is quite insufficient alone. Just as the Holy One altered salvation history by willing that the Word become flesh, so do ministers of the Gospel contribute to the effective unfolding of God's reign by proclaiming good news with sacred and authentic fervor.

Conclusion

At a hastily prepared news conference in August of 1996, Joseph Cardinal Bernardin of Chicago announced that his cancer had returned, that it was inoperable, and that his doctors advised him that he had less than a year to live. The previous year he had undergone surgery for pancreatic cancer followed by radiation treatment, but the cancer had spread to his liver and would soon take his life. He assured his listeners that he was at peace and welcomed death as a friend.

After his prepared remarks, he was asked an unusually personal question. A reporter respectfully wondered why he had made this tragic news public so quickly, when it is often shared only with family members. The Cardinal's response: "You are my family, and I am not speaking only of Catholics in Chicago." He then paused, smiled and added "And you'd find out anyway" (Steinfels 1996). He died three months later.

Bernardin often espoused what he called a "seamless garment" approach to life ethics. He borrowed the reference from the Gospel of John's mention of the woven tunic Jesus wore to his death (John 19:23). In response to the many contemporary challenges to the sanctity of human life—abortion, capital punishment, economic injustice, euthanasia—Bernardin believed that the proper response was a consistent ethic of life. He reasoned that the baptized could not be against abortion but in favor of capital punishment; rather, one championed the sanctity of human life against every threat. While an inspiring leader, Bernardin was not an especially flashy preacher. A selection of his published sermons reveals a thoughtful homilist whose measured remarks were well prepared but not great landmarks of homiletic literature. However, his preaching—and even his press conferences—revealed the weaving of its own kind of seamless garment. When wrongly accused of sexual abuse, he met the press with openness and consistency. When challenged for his progressive views by other leaders, even those inside the Church, he responded with respectful determination. Even when announcing his impending death, he spoke with calm assurance and even humor in both his prepared remarks and his necessary improvisations in light of the ensuing questions.

Like every leader, teacher, and preacher, Bernardin was flawed. He was also beloved. One basis of that belovedness, was the obvious coherence of his thinking and living, the believing, caring, strength, and humility that marked his ministry. Maybe that is why the cause for his canonization has been opened. In his own integrity, Bernardin models the particular promise and challenge of seamlessness for preachers. We are jugglers of doctrines and stories. We are purveyors of timeless truths and timely social critiques. We are stewards of the liturgy and servants of the Word. Moreover, we are commissioned to weave these various strands of knowing, believing, and feeling together in a persuasive and accessible homiletic performance week after week, and year after year so that it feeds the people of God and nourishes our own spirituality. It is a seamless garment few if any achieve, but one vital to pursue.

References

Foley, Edward. 2015. *Theological Reflection across Faith Traditions: The Turn to Reflective Believing*. New York: Rowman and Littlefield.

Gottschall, Jonathan. 2013. *The Storytelling Animal: How Stories Make Us Human*. Boston: Mariner Books.

Guttman, Leslie. 2011. "Important Strangers." In *This I Believe*. Ed. Dan Gediman, 142–144. Hoboken, NJ: John Wiley and Sons.

Kearney, Richard. 2002. *On Stories*. London: Routledge.

Lacey, Simon et al. 2017. "Engagement of the Left Extrastriate Body Area during Body-Part Metaphor Comprehension." *Brain and Language* 166: 1–18.

Lowry, Eugene. 2000. *The Homiletical Plot: The Sermon as Narrative Art Form*. Rev. ed. Louisville: Westminster John Knox Press.

McAdams, Dan. 2013. *The Redemptive Self. Stories Americans Live by*. Rev. ed. New York: Oxford University press.

Oatley, Keith. 2012. In "Your Brain on Fiction" by Annie Murphy Paul. *New York Times* (March 17, 2012).

Saliers, Don. 1994. "For the Sake of the World: Liturgy and Ethics." In his *Worship as Theology*. Nashville: Abingdon Press, 171–189.

Sapolsky, Robert. 2017. *Behave: The Biology of Humans at Our Best and Worst*. New York: Penguin.

Sexton, Anne. 1975. *An Awful Rowing toward God*. Boston: Houghton Mifflin.

Steinfels, Peter. 1996. "Cardinal Bernardin Says He Has Inoperable Cancer." *New York Times* (August 31, 1996): 6.

Wilder, Amos. 1969. *The New Voice: Religion, Literature, and Hermeneutics*. New York: Herder and Herder.

EPILOGUE

We're invited to pay attention
to the enchanted world around us
in a new way,
to be open to the possibility
of an encounter with God
at every moment.

~Mike Cosper

Anthony DeMello was a gifted storyteller. As the oldest son born into a Catholic family in pre-independence India, tradition dictated that he should he join the workforce like his father so that he could eventually support his family. At an early age, however, he expressed his desire to join the Jesuit community. The fortuitous and quite unexpected birth of a younger brother, thirteen years his junior, allowed Tony the freedom to pursue his dream. Over the relatively few remaining decades of his life—he died from a heart attack at age fifty-five—his dream blossomed into a unique gift for wedding the mystical traditions from the East and the West in a wise and welcoming manner. He had a particular gift for unpacking in fresh and fruitful ways the form of reflection St. Ignatius developed for his followers, known as the examen. Its five simple steps invite the practitioner to engage in thankful reflections about where and how God is present in our daily lives.

In these pages we have honored the spirit of Ignatius' counsel to see God in all things, and similar wisdom from other sources, as a particular and pressing mission for preachers. DeMello offers a simplified variation on this basic theme. While the term *examen* may evoke the specter of a penitential examination of conscience, DeMello and others provide a more gracious entry for those of us unfamiliar with this Ignatian practice. For him this is simply a prayer of and for awareness. De Mello explored the power of this awareness by drawing upon meditation practices from the East, simple exercises, and scriptural reflections. It is especially his brief wisdom tales, however, that make this point for me. A favorite is taken from his collection aptly titled *One Minute Wisdom*. He writes:

> As the Master grew old and infirm, the disciples begged
>   him not to die.
> Said the Master, "If I did not go, how would you ever see?"
> "What is it we fail to see when you are with us?" they asked.
> But the Master would not say.
> When the moment of his death was near, they said,
> "What is it we will see when you are gone?"
> With a twinkle in his eye, the Master said,
> "All I did was sit on the riverbank handing out river water.
> After I'm gone, I trust you will notice the river."
>
> (De Mello 1986, 89)

Preaching, like most ministries, can be both exhilarating and demoralizing. Some days, whole congregations are deeply moved by our words. There are even those rare moments when applause ripples across the assembly. The ensuing affirmations are intoxicating. Most days, however, the response is more tempered—even tepid. Our message is misunderstood, our exegesis questionable, our language uninspiring, and sometimes our hearts are clearly not invested in the task. That we choose to keep preaching, to continue engaging in the homiletic enterprise multiple times each week—for some, multiple times each Sunday—is nothing less than astounding.

While the pursuit of success can keep us motivated, success can be a problematic goal for ministry. In the eyes of the world, Jesus was not especially successful as a rabbi, and his whole effort for spiritual and moral reform seemed to have ended abruptly and disastrously at Golgotha. The Gospels, however, reveal a different motivation for the Son of God. His aim was not to be the center of adulation and unending hosannas. Rather, he was intent on bringing his followers to embrace the person and the peace of the One who sent him. Jesus was our original Master, stepping aside in his passion and death so that we might see the river and enter into its life-giving waters.

Paying attention to the many aspects of the ministry of preaching includes paying attention to how we perceive ourselves in this ministry. My self-understanding as a preacher has certainly evolved over the decades. Early on, I framed too much of my preaching as entertainment, symbolized by the almost incessant attempts to inject humor into the homily. Over the years that approach has largely evaporated, partly because the humor never seemed to draw people deeper into the mystery and partly because the preaching task increasingly demanded more of me personally. One of those demands was more authenticity. For me this translated into a willingness to reveal my own vulnerability and even confusion about my faith, Church, and self in tumultuous and terrifying times, from the shame of the sexual abuse crisis through the panic of the COVID-19 pandemic. On the journey, I discover that, like other preachers, I am one who needs to see the river and not just hand out river water. Preaching has become personally pivotal for entering this river, a difficult but cherished path for journeying into the mystery of God. What began as a ministerial task has now become a deeply spiritual exercise.

Whatever the stage of your preaching journey, whatever the path you and your community are taking toward that holy river, may you stay attentive to the wonder, alert to the Spirit, and grateful for every clue of divinity you stumble across. Each day we begin again, as the poet advises: pay attention, be astonished, tell about it, through Christ our Lord.

References

Cosper, Mike. 2017. *Recapturing the Wonder: Transcendent Faith in a Disenchanted World*. Westmont, IL: InterVarsity Press.

De Mello, Anthony. 1986. *One Minute Wisdom*. New York: Image–Doubleday.

INDEX

Dance 69, 99, 102, 104, 106, 107
De Mello, Anthony 138–140
Deacons 37, 38, 45, 50, 52, 53
Death 6, 31, 35, 56, 63, 64, 71, 89, 97, 106,
      113, 131, 135, 136, 139–140
   as a dance with God 106
   also see Crucifixion,
      Paschal mystery
Dialogue vi, 10, 11, 13, 19, 20, 21, 42, 72,
      79, 90
   preaching as 11, 13, 18, 19, 20
   also see Interfaith
Disability 44
Disciples 5, 6, 7, 8, 9, 17, 18, 43, 44
   also see Evangelization, Mission
Discipleship 40, 52, 81, 83
Discipline 2, 12, 16, 134
Discrimination 36, 41, 44
   also see Hate Crimes, Racism,
     Them-ing, Violence
Diversity 29, 34, 37, 41, 85, 86, 97, 109
   also see Context, Ethnicity, Race
Dogma, dogmatics vi, viii, 13, 52, 123
   also see Church teaching, Ethics
Drama:
   Mass Appeal 45, 46
   Oedipus Rex 128
Dramatists:
   Bill Davis, 46
   Sophocles 128
Dreyfus, Hubert and Stuart 14, 15, 23
Ecclesiology
   humility based
   also see Church
Educators 1, 28, 38, 41, 98
   religious educators 38
Emotions, see Affect
Empathy 11, 12, 13 , 14, 23, 33, 36, 45, 97,
     120, 121, 131
Encounter
   preaching as vii, 6, 13, 18, 33, 35, 52,
     121, 122, 123, 140
   also see Homily
Equilibrium 130, 132
   oops 130, 131,

   upsetting 130, 132
   also see Preachers: Eugene Lowry
Ethics vi, 12, 19, 31, 84, 125, 136, 137
   Consistent ethic of life 135
   seamless garment 136
Ethnicity 31, 34, 35, 44
   also see African-American,
     Hispanic, Latinx, Native
     American, Race
Ethnography 27, 28, 29, 30, 32, 38, 39, 46,
     47, 131
   humility based 27
   pastoral 29, 39, 131
Eucharist 20, 44, 51, 57, 58, 63, 90, 125
   Eucharistic Prayers 17, 54, 64, 67,
     90, 112,
   Prefaces 64, 67, 90
   also see Bread and Wine, Liturgy,
     Sunday Mass
Evangelization 8, 18, 125
   also see Apologetics, Mission,
     Unaffiliated, Witness
Exegesis 6, 40, 57, 58, 60, 69, 133, 139
Feelings, see Affect
Fiction 92, 96, 111, 120, 137
   also see Literature, Novels,
     Storytelling
Foolishness 104
Francis, Pope 8, 10, 12, 13, 18, 19, 21, 23,
     27, 30, 32, 33, 36, 42, 46, 76, 78
Francis, St. 46, 76
Fulfilled in Your Hearing 53, 30
Funerals 19, 20, 21, 61
Gender 29, 35, 36, 37, 38, 41, 43, 44, 46
   roles
   shifting gender boundaries 41
   also see LGBTQ, Sexuality,
     Transgender, Women
Generational cohort, see Age cohort
Generosity, generous 23, 43, 121
God, *passim*
   as storyteller 119,
   our paying attention to 2, 7, 78, 79, 80,
     84, 89, 90, 104

sense imagery vii
watching our language 13, 20, 38
  also see Rhetoric,
Last Supper 6, 125
also, see Eucharist
Latinx 14, 44
  also see Hispanic
Lectionary, *passim*
and billiards 58, 59
Catholic principle of 60
Introduction to 61, 67
Revised Common Lectionary 52
  also see Scripture
LGBTQ community 42
  also see Gender, Matthew Shepard,
    Transgender
Liberation 131
liberation theology 15
Liquid 8
liquid modernity 42
  also see Philosophers:
    Zygmunt Bauman
Listening 32, 33, 38, 42, 45, 78, 79, 81,
    118, 135
audio books 102
to women 38
to young adults 32
  also see Paying attention
Literature vii, 41, 81, 91, 136, 137
plot twists in 128
  also see Art, Biography, Fiction,
    Memoir, Novels, Poetry
Liturgical Year, see Church Year
Liturgy, liturgical, *passim*
committee 30
gestures 57, 58, 64, 69
music vi, 56, 57, 98, 105
texts 10, 112
theology 56, 70, 137
of the Church vii, 51, 52
of the Word 53, 97
of the world 18, 53, 60, 61, 65
  also see Eucharist, Occasional
    services, Propers, Ritual, Sacred
    Texts, Worship

Local 6, 8, 9, 18, 30, 41, 44, 51, 67, 68,
    118, 119
church 18, 34, 45
need 18, 67
  also see Context
Location 2, 34
social location 34
  also see Context
Love, *passim*
of God 14, 76, 108
of the other 14, 87, 89, 121
Mandela, Nelson 90
Marginalized 5, 28, 104, 135
  also see Poor
Marriage 90
Mary, Blessed Virgin 32, 40, 106
  also see Annunciation
Mass 21, 50, 54, 60, 66, 90
attending 10, 32, 56
Sunday 50
  also see Eucharist
Media 23, 30, 78, 98, 112, 115, 129
cool 111
hot 111
  also see Internet, Movies, Social
    Communication, Technology
Memoir 95, 96, 111
Memorial 50, 51, 63, 64
Men 32, 37, 38, 40, 45, 113, 114
  also see Gender
Mercy 19, 44, 54, 87, 110
Method 15, 24, 27, 28, 67, 76, 82, 121, 133
for preaching 15, 33, 134
methodological laziness 28
  also see Preachers: Eugene Lowry,
    Theological Reflection
Ministry vi, 3, 4, 28, 38, 41, 73, 118, 120,
    136, 139–140
practices of vii, viii, 12, 15, 20, 78,
    81, 91, 103, 104, 125, 129, 134,
    135, 139–140
Mission 18, 19, 41, 42, 44, 58, 65, 75, 89,
    101, 106, 123, 125, 129, 138
missionary disciples
  also see Evangelization, Witness

Pulpit, *passim*
  ambo 125
  lectern 68, 69, 70
Race 31, 34, 35, 36, 337, 44, 68, 95, 96
  also see African American,
    Ethnicity, Hispanic, Latinx,
    Native American
Racism 34, 35, 36, 80, 95, 97
  also see Authors: Ta-Nehisi Coates,
    Discrimination Them-ing
Reflection, *passim*
  also see Contemplation,
    Theological Reflection
Reformation 52
  also see Lectionary, Scripture
Respect 4, 5, 12, 33, 56, 76, 98, 113, 118
Resurrection 20, 44, 63, 64, 81, 103, 132
  also see Paschal mystery
Revelation, *passim*
  auditory nature of 81
  creation as 43, 56, 76, 84, 89, 90, 105,
    114, 121, 123
  also see Scripture, Second
    Vatican Council,
Rhetoric 40, 49, 119, 123, 124
  ethos 124
  pathos 124
  also see Language
Rite of Christian Initiation of Adults 61
  also see Initiation
Ritual 13, 21, 28
  dance 62, 102
  gestures 57, 58, 64, 69, 103
  also see Liturgy
Roman Missal vii, 54, 60, 65, 66, 68
*General Instruction of the Roman
    Missal* 66, 67
  also see Propers
Sacrament 56, 57, 63, 70, 75
  Church as 75
  sacramental principle 75
  also see Baptism, Eucharist,
    Imagination (sacramental),
    Sacramentality
Sacramentality 56, 74, 75, 76, 118
  of the world 55, 57, 75, 76, 118

sacramentals 56
  also see Sacrament
Sacred text 53, 54 62, 64, 65, 66, 69
  also see Liturgy, Propers,
    Roman Missal
Samaritans 5, 6, 43, 86, 87, 90, 91, 104,
    121, 122
Sapolsky, Robert 11, 24, 35, 36, 47, 128, 137
Science, *passim*
  astronomy 74
  bioacoustics 78
  biology 24, 78, 137
  chemistry 73, 74, 76
  engineering 78, 91, 129
  entomology 9, 74
  ethnography 27, 28, 29, 38, 39, 46,
    47, 131
  in theological curricula 73
  mathematics 105
  medicine 15, 31, 95, 102, 103, 115
  meteorology 85, 108
  neuroscience 74, 82, 83
  paleontology 82
  psychology 25, 87, 88
  social science 88, 118
  zoology 78
Scientists:
  Alfred Adler 11
  Christopher Chabris 25, 26, 46
  Nicholaus Copernicus 71, 72, 73
  Albert Einstein 72, 77
  Robert Emmons 88, 89
  Richard Feynman 104
  Galileo Galilei 71, 72, 73
  Clifford Geertz 28
  Andrew Greeley 55, 56, 69, 93
  Stephen Hawking 77
  Jaroslav Hynecek 72, 93
  Wes Jackson 27, 46
  Friedrich August Kekulé 92
  Johannes Kepler 105
  Edward Lorenz 85
  Dan McAdams 120, 137
  John Money 41
  Keith Oatley 120, 137

SCRIPTURAL REFERENCES

"Many a preacher longs for a 'how to' manual, wanting to become one of those spellbinding ministers who can break open the Word in ways that lead hearers into beauty, awe, holy mystery into the very heart of God while connecting the dots of graced encounter of peoples' daily realities. Ed Foley is such a preacher. Every minister of the Word will want to learn from his wisdom gleaned through a lifetime of attending and reflecting, gathered into this gem of a book."

Barbara E. Reid, OP
President and Carroll Stuhlmueller, CP,
    Distinguished Professor of New Testament Studies
Catholic Theological Union

"In this wise book, Foley inspires preachers to witness to Christ in our midst and God at work in the chaos of life by turning their attention not away from but beyond lectionary, liturgy, and Church to sacredly notice God present in the great and small moments of life. Foley demonstrates how God, present in art, film, poetry, and science, enlivens sermon preparation and renders the Gospel more relevant so the assembly expects to encounter the divine in everyday life. Yet the true gift of this book is a scholar and teacher who never ceased to be preacher and priest, welcoming us into a ministry and process he obviously loves."

Craig Alan Satterlee
Bishop in the Evangelical Lutheran Church in America
Former teacher of preaching at Lutheran School of
    Theology at Chicago and the University of Notre Dame